Nice & Easy Desserts
COOKBOOK

by Cyndee Kannenberg

Ideals Publishing Corp.
Milwaukee, Wisconsin

CONTENTS

Chart of Equivalents

Almonds, sliced	1 cup	3½-oz. can
Almonds, slivered	1 cup	4-oz. can
Apples, sliced	4 cups	4 medium
Banana, mashed	1 cup	3 medium
Cottage Cheese	1 cup	8 oz.
Cream cheese	6 tablespoons	3 oz.
Chocolate, semisweet chips	1 cup	6-oz. pkg.
Chocolate, unsweetened	1 square	1 oz.
Citron	½ cup	4-oz. pkg.
Cream, heavy	1 cup whipped	½ cup
Cream, sour	1 cup	8 oz.
Currants, dried	2 cups	11 oz.
Dates, pitted and chopped	1¼ cups	8 oz.
Graham cracker crumbs	1 cup	12 squares
Lemon juice	3 tablespoons	1 large lemon
Lemon peel, grated	1½ teaspoons	1 lemon
Milk, evaporated	⅔ cup	6-oz. can
Orange juice	1 cup	3 medium oranges
Orange peel, grated	1 teaspoon	½ orange
Peaches, fresh, sliced	4 cups	8 peaches
Peanuts, chopped	1½ cups	6¾-oz. can
Pecans, shelled	1 cup	3-oz. can
Raisins	3 cups	15-oz. pkg.
Rhubarb, 1 inch pieces	3 cups	1 lb.
Strawberries, sliced	2 cups	1 pt.
Sugar, brown, firmly packed	2¼ cups	1-lb. box
Sugar, confectioners', unsifted	4 cups	1-lb. box
Sugar, granulated	2⅓ cups	1 lb.
Walnuts	1 cup	4-oz. can

ISBN 0-89542-612-9

COPYRIGHT © MCMLXXVIII BY CYNDEE KANNENBERG
PUBLISHED BY IDEALS PUBLISHING CORPORATION
MILWAUKEE, WISCONSIN 53226
ALL RIGHTS RESERVED. PRINTED AND BOUND IN U.S.A.
PUBLISHED SIMULTANEOUSLY IN CANADA

CAKES

CANDY BAR POUND CAKE

8 1¾-oz. Milky Way candy bars
1 c. butter
2 c. sugar
4 eggs
2½ c. sifted flour
½ t. baking soda
1¼ c. buttermilk
1 t. vanilla
1 c. chopped nuts

Combine candy bars and ½ cup of the butter in a saucepan; melt over low heat. Cream sugar with remaining ½ cup butter. Add eggs, one at a time, beating well after each addition. Stir together flour and baking soda. Add alternately with buttermilk, stirring until smooth. Add melted candy; mix well. Stir in the vanilla and nuts. Pour into a greased and floured bundt pan and bake in a 350° oven for 75 to 80 minutes. Cool and frost with Candy Icing. Serves 16 to 20.

CANDY ICING

3 fun-size Milky Way candy bars
½ c. butter
2 c. sifted confectioners' sugar
1 t. vanilla
Milk

Melt candy bars in butter. Add sugar and vanilla. Blend in just enough milk to make of spreading consistency.

Before melting chocolate, brush inside of the pan with melted butter. The chocolate will not stick to the pan.

CANDY BAR CAKE

8 1⅕-oz. milk chocolate bars
1 c. butter
2 c. sugar
4 eggs
¼ t. baking soda
1 c. buttermilk
1 5½-oz. can chocolate syrup
2 t. vanilla
2½ c. flour
½ t. salt
1 c. chopped nuts

Melt chocolate bars in top of a double boiler. Remove from heat. Cream melted chocolate, butter and sugar. Add eggs, one at a time. Dissolve soda in buttermilk. Add to the chocolate mixture. Mix in syrup and vanilla and then flour, salt and nuts. Pour into a greased tube pan. Bake in a 350° oven 75 minutes. Cool 10 minutes. Turn out of pan. Cake freezes well. Serves 16.

TREASURE TOFFEE CAKE

¼ c. sugar
1 t. cinnamon
2 c. flour
1 c. sugar
1½ t. baking powder
1 t. baking soda
¼ t. salt
1 t. vanilla
1 c. sour cream
½ c. butter, softened
2 eggs
¼ c. chopped nuts
3 1⅛-oz. chocolate toffee bars, coarsely crushed
¼ c. melted butter
Confectioners' sugar

Combine cinnamon and sugar. In mixer, combine remaining ingredients except nuts, candy bars and melted butter. Blend at low speed until moistened. Beat at medium speed 3 minutes. Spoon half of the batter into greased and floured 10-inch bundt pan. Sprinkle with 2 tablespoons cinnamon-sugar mixture. Spoon remaining mixture into pan. Top with remaining cinnamon-sugar mixture. Top with nuts and chopped candy. Pour melted butter over all. Bake in a 325° oven 45 to 50 minutes. Cool upright 15 minutes. Remove from pan and dust with confectioners' sugar. Serves 16.

HIDDEN TREASURE CAKE

    1 c. butter
2½ c. sugar
    4 eggs
    2 t. vanilla
    4 c. sifted cake flour
    1 T. baking soda
    1 t. salt
    1 c. milk
    1 8-oz. carton lemon yogurt
       Grated rind of 1 lemon
       Juice of 1 lemon

Cream butter until light. Slowly add sugar, beating until fluffy. Add eggs, one at a time, beating well after each addition; add vanilla. Sift together flour, soda and salt. Add dry ingredients alternately with milk and yogurt, beginning and ending with dry ingredients. Blend in lemon juice and rind. Pour batter into lightly greased and floured 10-inch tube pan. Bake in a 350° oven about 70 minutes or until done. Cool upright on wire rack for 10 minutes. Turn out to cool for about 2 hours. Fill and ice. Serves 12.

FILLING

    1 3-oz. pkg. raspberry gelatin
    1 c. boiling water
    2 8-oz. cartons plain yogurt

Dissolve gelatin in boiling water. Chill until thickened slightly. Add yogurt and blend until smooth. Refrigerate 10 to 15 minutes. Remove center of cake by cutting ¾ inch from outside edge and ¾ inch in from the center hole, cutting within 1 inch of bottom. Carefully remove inside cake in sections, leaving only a shell. Place shell on serving plate. Spoon Filling into shell. Replace cake sections on top of the raspberry mixture to fill center. Refrigerate 30 minutes.

ICING

    ⅓ c. butter
    1 1-lb. box confectioners' sugar
    ⅓ c. lemon juice
    2 t. vanilla
    1 t. butter flavoring
       Grated rind of 1 lemon
       Whole raspberries for garnish

Cream butter. Slowly beat in sugar, alternating with lemon juice. Stir in vanilla, butter flavoring and lemon rind. Garnish with whole raspberries.

WELLESLEY FUDGE CAKE

    3 1-oz. squares unsweetened chocolate, melted
2½ c. flour
    1 t. baking soda
    ½ t. salt
    ½ c. butter
    2 c. brown sugar
    2 eggs
    ½ t. vanilla
    ½ c. milk
    ½ c. water

Melt chocolate over double boiler. Sift together flour, soda and salt; set aside. Cream butter and sugar until fluffy. Beat in eggs and vanilla. Add melted chocolate. Combine milk and water and add to mixture alternately with sifted dry ingredients. Pour into 2 greased and floured 9-inch pans. Bake in a 350° oven 30 to 35 minutes. Serves 12.

FUDGE ICING

    2 c. brown sugar
    ½ c. milk
    3 1-oz. squares chocolate, melted
    2 T. butter

Combine all ingredients, mixing until of spreading consistency.

CHOCOLATE CAKE ROLL

    ½ c. sifted cake flour
    ¾ t. baking powder
    ¼ t. salt
    3 eggs, beaten
    ½ c. sugar
    1 t. almond flavoring
    1 T. confectioners' sugar
    ½ pkg. dietetic chocolate pudding
1½ c. skim milk
    2 T. toasted chopped pecans

Lightly butter jelly-roll pan. Line with waxed paper and lightly butter paper. Sift together flour, baking powder and salt; set aside. Beat eggs well. Add granulated sugar, a little at a time, beating until thick. Add flavoring. Fold in flour mixture. Pour in pan. Bake in a 400° oven 8 minutes. Loosen cake edges with a knife. Turn out on waxed paper dusted with confectioners' sugar. Peel off waxed paper. Roll up cake, starting at the shorter end; cool. Prepare pudding as directed on the box, using only 1½ cups milk. Add pecans; chill. Unroll cake. Spread with pudding. Reroll and sprinkle with confectioners' sugar. Serves 10.

MOCHA CUPCAKES

½ c. sugar
6 T. butter
1 egg
1 egg yolk
1 1-oz. square unsweetened chocolate,
  melted and cooled
1 c. flour
1 t. baking powder
¼ t. salt
¼ t. baking soda
1 T. instant coffee crystals
½ c. milk

Cream sugar and butter; beat in egg and egg yolk until fluffy. Add chocolate. Sift together flour, baking powder, salt and baking soda. Dissolve coffee crystals in milk. Add dry ingredients to chocolate mixture, alternating with milk mixture. Fill 12 paper-lined muffin pans two-thirds full with batter. Bake in a preheated 275° oven 12 minutes. Spoon 1 tablespoon Meringue on top of each cupcake. Bake an additional 10 to 12 minutes until lightly browned. Makes 12 cupcakes.

MOCHA MERINGUE

1 egg white
1 t. instant coffee crystals
⅓ c. sugar
½ c. semisweet chocolate chips
½ c. chopped pecans

Beat egg white with coffee crystals until soft peaks form. Gradually add sugar, beating to stiff peaks. Fold in chocolate chips and nuts.

SOUP CAKE

¾ c. shortening
1½ c. sugar
3 eggs
3 c. sifted flour
1 T. baking powder
1 t. baking soda
1 t. cloves
1 t. cinnamon
1 t. nutmeg
1 10½-oz. can tomato soup
⅓ c. milk
1 c. raisins
1 c. chopped nuts

Cream sugar and shortening until fluffy. Add eggs and blend. Use ¼ cup of the flour and toss with raisins and nuts. Sift together dry ingredients and set aside. Combine tomato soup and milk, blending well. Add dry ingredients to creamed mixture, alternating with soup. Fold in nuts and raisins. Pour into a greased and floured 12-cup bundt pan. Bake in a 350° oven 50 minutes or until done. Cool in pan 15 minutes. Turn onto wire rack to finish cooling. Glaze. Serves 24.

GLAZE

2 c. sifted confectioners' sugar
1 T. softened butter
½ t. pumpkin pie spice
2 to 4 T. milk

Mix first three ingredients. Slowly add milk and mix to spreading consistency.

BLACK FOREST CAKE

4 eggs
¾ t. vanilla
⅔ c. sugar
⅓ c. cocoa
⅓ c. sifted flour
6 T. clarified butter
½ c. sugar
¾ c. water
¼ c. kirsch
1 c. pitted dark cherries, drained
2 c. heavy cream, whipped
⅓ c. confectioners' sugar
1 4-oz. bar semisweet chocolate, shaved
  in curls
Maraschino cherries for garnish

Combine eggs, vanilla and two-thirds cup sugar; beat with electric mixer 10 minutes at high speed. Sift together flour and cocoa; fold into egg mixture. Add melted butter, stirring just until mixed. Do not overmix. Pour into 3 greased and floured 6-inch round pans. Bake in a 350° oven 10 to 15 minutes. Cool 5 minutes. Remove from pans and cool on racks. In a saucepan, combine ½ cup sugar and water; boil 5 minutes. Cool to lukewarm and add kirsch. Sprinkle over cake layers. Fold confectioners' sugar into whipped cream. Spread 1 cake layer with cream, sprinkle on half the cherries. Repeat with second layer then add top layer. Frost top and sides of cake with remaining whipped cream and garnish with maraschino cherries and shaved chocolate. Serves 8.

Pictured oppos
Black Forest C

PUMPKIN CUPCAKES

3 c. flour
1 c. sugar
4 t. baking powder
1 t. salt
1 t. pumpkin pie spice
1 c. milk
1 c. canned pumpkin
½ c. melted butter
2 eggs, beaten

Sift together flour, sugar, baking powder, salt and pumpkin pie spice. Stir in milk, pumpkin, melted butter and eggs. Use a wooden spoon to mix just until the batter is moist. Pour batter into 24 well-greased muffin cups, 2½ inches in diameter. Bake in a preheated 400° oven for 20 minutes. Cool in tins 10 minutes. Loosen muffins and invert pan on a wire rack. Makes 24 cupcakes.

HOLIDAY CAKE

1 8-oz. pkg. cream cheese, softened
1 c. butter or margarine
1½ c. sugar
1 t. vanilla
4 eggs
2¼ c. sifted cake flour
1½ t. baking powder
1 c. chopped candied fruit
1 c. chopped pecans
Cherries for garnish
Pecans for garnish

Blend cream cheese, butter, sugar and vanilla. Mix well. Add eggs, one at a time, mixing well after each. Sift together 2 cups flour and baking powder. Gradually add to cream cheese mixture. Combine remaining flour with the candied fruit and half the nuts. Fold into the batter. Grease a bundt pan. Sprinkle remaining nuts over the inside of pan. Pour batter in pan and bake in a preheated 325° oven for about 1 hour and 20 minutes. Cool 10 minutes. Remove from pan. Pour Glaze over and garnish with pecans and cherries. Serves 16.

GLAZE

1½ c. sifted confectioners' sugar
2 T. milk
¼ t. vanilla

Stir milk and vanilla into confectioners' sugar, stirring well.

CHOCOLATE CHERRY FRUITCAKE

2 c. chopped candied cherries
1 c. raisins
1 c. chopped dates
1 c. chopped walnuts
½ c. flour
½ c. butter
½ c. sugar
2 eggs
¾ c. flour
¼ c. cocoa
½ t. baking powder
½ t. salt
⅓ c. buttermilk
Kirsch

Combine cherries, raisins, dates and nuts with ½ cup flour. Set aside. Cream butter and sugar until fluffy. Add eggs, beating well. Stir together remaining flour, cocoa, baking powder and salt. Add to creamed mixture, alternating with buttermilk. Fold in fruit and nut mixture. Pour into 2 greased 8 x 4 x 2-inch loaf pans. Bake in a 275° oven 1½ to 1¾ hours. Cool in pan 10 minutes. Turn out on wire rack and cool completely. Wrap in a kirsch-soaked cheesecloth and then in foil. Store in a cool place from 1 week to 6 months. Resoak cloth once a week. Chill before serving. Serves 10 to 12.

MOTHER-IN-LAW'S DATE CAKE

1 c. dates, cut up
1 t. baking soda
1¼ c. boiling water
¾ c. shortening
1 c. sugar
2 beaten eggs
1¼ c. plus 2 T. flour
¾ t. baking powder
1 t. salt
1 6-oz. pkg. chocolate chips
¼ c. sugar
½ c. chopped nuts

Stir soda into boiling water; pour over dates and set aside. Cream shortening and 1 cup sugar until fluffy. Stir in eggs, mixing well. Add dates. Sift together flour, baking powder and salt. Add to date mixture. Pour batter into a greased and floured 9 x 13-inch pan. Combine chocolate chips, remaining sugar and nuts. Sprinkle over top of cake. Bake in a preheated 350° oven 35 to 40 minutes (use 325° for glass pans). Serves 12.

TANGY FRUITCAKE

½ c. butter
¾ c. sugar
2 eggs
1 T. lemon rind
1 t. lemon extract
1⅔ c. sifted cake flour
1½ t. baking powder
¼ t. salt
⅔ c. milk
  Confectioners' sugar
  Sliced and sweetened strawberries
  Heavy cream, whipped

Cream butter and sugar until light and fluffy. Beat in eggs, one at a time, beating well after each addition. Add lemon rind and extract. Sift together flour, salt and baking powder. Add dry ingredients alternately with milk, beating with mixer at medium speed. Begin and end with dry ingredients. Pour batter into a greased and floured 6½-cup ring mold. Bake in a 325° oven for 30 to 40 minutes. Cool on wire rack for 10 minutes. Loosen edges and invert. Sprinkle with confectioners' sugar. Fill center with strawberries and top with whipped cream. Serves 10 to 12.

ORANGE RUM CAKE

2⅔ c. sifted cake flour
2½ t. baking powder
½ t. salt
¼ t. baking soda
  Pinch ginger
⅔ c. butter
1⅓ c. sugar
3 egg yolks
1½ t. grated orange rind
¾ c. orange juice
¼ c. rum
½ t. almond extract
½ t. vanilla
3 egg whites, beaten stiff
  Confectioners' sugar

Sift together first 5 ingredients twice. Cream butter until light. Gradually add sugar, creaming until fluffy. Add egg yolks, one at a time, beating well after each. Stir in orange rind. Add dry ingredients alternately with orange juice mixed with rum. Beat well; stir in almond extract and vanilla. Fold in egg whites and pour into a buttered 10-inch tube pan. Bake in a 350° oven 45 to 60 minutes. Serve sprinkled with confectioners' sugar. Serves 12 to 14.

GREAT-GRANDMA'S RAISIN CAKE

1 t. baking soda
1 c. boiling water
1 c. raisins
2 c. flour
½ t. baking powder
½ c. shortening
1 c. sugar
1 egg
½ c. chopped nuts

Dissolve soda in boiling water and pour over raisins. Set aside to cool. Sift together flour and baking powder. Add to raisin mixture. Cream shortening and sugar. Beat in egg and add to raisin mixture. Stir in nuts. Pour in a greased 9 x 5-inch loaf pan. Bake in a 350° oven 60 minutes. Serves 10 to 12.

PEANUT CANDY CAKE

1¾ c. boiling water
1 c. quick-cooking rolled oats
½ c. butter
1 c. light brown sugar, packed
1 c. sugar
1 t. vanilla
2 eggs
1½ c. flour
1 t. baking soda
½ t. baking powder
¼ t. cinnamon
¼ t. salt
5 .6-oz. chocolate peanut butter cup candies

Combine water and oats; mix well. Cool to room temperature. Cream butter, brown sugar, sugar and vanilla. Beat in eggs, then oatmeal mixture. Sift together dry ingredients and add; beat 1 minute. Pour batter into a greased and floured 9 x 13-inch pan. Crumble candies and sprinkle on top, having a thicker layer around the edges. Bake in a 350° oven 40 to 45 minutes until done. Frost with Chocolate Icing. Serves 12.

ICING

½ c. cocoa
2⅔ c. confectioners' sugar
6 T. butter
⅛ t. salt
4 to 5 T. milk
1 t. vanilla

Combine cocoa and sugar. Cream butter and salt with one-third of the cocoa mixture. Gradually add milk, vanilla and remaining cocoa mixture. Beat until smooth.

APPLE CAKE

1 T. butter
½ c. sugar
2 c. flour
2 t. baking powder
1 egg plus milk to make 1 cup
6 to 8 apples, peeled and sliced

Combine butter, sugar, flour and baking powder; stir well. Add milk and egg, mixing to blend. Spread in 2 greased and floured 8-inch pans. Cover with apple slices. Sprinkle Topping over apples and, if desired, coconut or cinnamon on the top. Bake in a preheated 375° oven for 30 minutes. Makes two 8-inch cakes, or stack layers for one cake.

TOPPING

2 T. flour
1 c. sugar
2 T. melted butter

Mix all ingredients together with a fork.

ECONOMICAL CARROT CAKE

3 eggs
2 c. sugar
1 c. vegetable oil
1 t. salt
1 t. baking powder
1 t. baking soda
1 t. cinnamon
1 t. vanilla
½ t. nutmeg
⅛ t. cloves
3 c. flour
2 c. shredded carrot
¼ c. milk

Measure all ingredients except flour, carrot and milk into a large mixing bowl. Beat ½ minute on low speed; beat on medium speed for 1 minute. Gradually stir in flour, carrot and milk. Pour into two greased and floured 10-inch cake pans. Bake in a 350° oven 30 to 35 minutes. Cool in pan 10 to 15 minutes. Remove from pan and cool on rack. Makes 16 servings.

CREAM CHEESE ICING

2 c. confectioners' sugar
1 3-oz. pkg. cream cheese, softened
1 T. milk
1 t. vanilla

Combine all ingredients in a small bowl. Beat on medium speed until smooth and of spreading consistency, about 3 minutes.

MERINGUE CAKE

4 egg whites
¼ t. cream of tartar
1 c. sugar
½ c. finely chopped pecans
1 1-oz. square unsweetened chocolate, grated
1 c. sugar
½ c. butter
1½ t. vanilla
4 egg yolks
2 c. sifted cake flour
3 t. baking powder
½ t. salt
¾ c. milk

Grease a 10-inch tube pan. Line the bottom with waxed paper. Beat egg whites and cream of tartar at medium high speed until soft peaks form. Gradually add the first cup of sugar, beating at high speed until stiff peaks form. Gently fold in chocolate and pecans. Spread meringue evenly over the bottom and 3½ inches up the sides and center of the tube. Set aside. Cream remaining sugar, butter and vanilla until fluffy. Add egg yolks, one at a time, beating well after each addition. Sift together flour, baking powder and salt. Add to the creamed mixture alternately with the milk, beating well after each addition. Carefully spoon into the meringue-lined pan. Bake in a 325° oven 55 to 60 minutes. Do not invert pan. Cool in pan on rack 20 minutes. Loosen around sides and center tube; invert on cake rack to cool completely. Serves 16.

ORANGE RIND CAKE

1 c. raisins
½ c. nuts
Rind of 2 oranges
1 c. sugar
½ c. butter
2 eggs
1 c. buttermilk
1 t. baking soda
2½ c. flour

Put raisins, nuts and rind through a grinder. Set aside. Cream butter with sugar; stir in eggs and buttermilk, mixing well. Add soda, flour and ground mixture. Pour batter into a greased and floured bundt pan. Bake in a 350° oven 45 to 60 minutes. Serves 10 to 12. Frost with Fudgy Chocolate Icing, page 18.

ctured opposite:
pple Cake

CHEESE TOPPED PINEAPPLE CAKE

2 8-oz. pkgs. cream cheese, softened
½ c. sugar
1 t. vanilla
1 egg
1 pkg. pineapple or lemon cake mix
2 eggs
1 c. water
1 16-oz. pkg. frozen strawberries, thawed

Cream 1½ packages cream cheese until fluffy. Gradually add sugar, vanilla and 1 egg. Beat well. Spread mixture evenly in a greased and lightly floured 9 x 13-inch pan. Blend cake mix, remaining cream cheese, 2 eggs and water; beat 4 minutes. Spread over cheese mixture. Bake in a 350° oven 40 to 50 minutes until a toothpick inserted in the middle comes out clean. Cool in pan 5 minutes. Remove from pan and cool completely. Cut into 12 pieces and serve topped with strawberries. Serves 12.

COLA CAKE

1 c. butter, softened
1⅓ c. sugar
2 eggs
2 c. flour
1 t. baking soda
3 T. cocoa
½ c. buttermilk
1 t. vanilla
1 c. cola
1½ c. miniature marshmallows

Cream butter and sugar until fluffy. Add eggs, one at a time, beating after each. Sift together flour, baking soda, cocoa and add, alternating with buttermilk. Stir in vanilla and cola, blending well. Fold in marshmallows. Pour into a 13 x 9-inch well-greased pan. Bake in a 350° oven 40 to 45 minutes. Cool and frost with Cola Icing. Serves 12.

COLA ICING

4 c. confectioners' sugar
½ c. softened butter
3 T. cocoa
⅓ c. cola
1 c. chopped pecans (optional)

Cream sugar, butter and cocoa. Add cola, beating until smooth. Stir in pecans. Makes 12 servings.

SPECKLED BANANA CAKE

1 pkg. yellow cake mix
1 c. hot water
½ c. vegetable oil
1 3-oz. pkg. instant banana pudding mix
4 eggs
¼ c. poppy seed

Mix cake mix, water, oil and dry pudding mix. Beat until smooth. Add eggs, one at a time, beating well after each addition. Stir in poppy seed. Pour batter into greased and floured tube pan. Bake in a preheated 350° oven 45 minutes. Serves 16.

Mix a tablespoonful of gelatin powder into a thawed package of frozen berries. Stir well. Use as a topping for sherbets or plain cake.

FAVORITE CAKE

3 c. sifted cake flour
4 t. baking powder
¼ t. salt
1 c. butter
2 c. sugar
1 t. vanilla
4 eggs
1 c. milk

Have all ingredients at room temperature. Sift flour three times with baking powder and salt. Cream butter thoroughly, using medium speed of mixer; add sugar gradually. Cream well; add vanilla. Add eggs, one at a time, beating well after each. Using low speed of mixer, add dry ingredients, alternating with milk. Pour into 2 greased and floured 9-inch pans. Bake in a 375° oven 25 minutes. Frost with Fluffy Custard Frosting. Serves 12.

FLUFFY CUSTARD FROSTING

2 T. flour
¾ c. milk
¾ c. butter
¾ c. sugar
⅛ t. salt
1 t. vanilla

In a saucepan, add a small amount of milk to flour. Stir, making a smooth paste. Add remaining milk. Cook over medium heat, stirring constantly, until mixture boils and thickens. Cool. Cream butter, using medium speed of mixer. Gradually add sugar and salt; beat well. Add cooled milk mixture. Whip until light and fluffy. Add vanilla.

FEATHER CAKE

    2 c. sifted cake flour
    3 t. baking powder
    ½ t. salt
    ½ c. butter
    1 c. sugar
    1 t. vanilla
    4 egg whites
    ½ c. milk

Have ingredients at room temperature. Sift flour, baking powder and salt 3 times. Cream butter thoroughly, using medium speed of the mixer. Slowly add sugar and cream well. Add vanilla and egg whites, one at a time, beating well after each. Using low speed of the mixer, add sifted dry ingredients alternately with milk. Pour into 2 greased 8-inch pans. Bake in a preheated 375° oven for 20 minutes. Cool. Put layers together with Nut Filling. Ice with a boiled icing. Serves 10.

NUT FILLING

    ½ c. sugar
    ¼ t. salt
    2½ T. flour
    1 c. milk
    1 egg, beaten
    ½ t. vanilla
    ⅓ c. chopped nuts

Combine sugar, salt and flour; add milk. Cook over low heat or in top of double boiler until thick. Pour slowly over beaten egg, stirring constantly. Simmer another 2 to 3 minutes. Cool and add vanilla and nuts.

ANGEL DESSERT

    2 T. unflavored gelatin
    4 T. cold water
    1 c. boiling water
    1 c. orange juice
    2 T. lemon juice
    1 c. sugar
    ⅛ t. salt
    1 pt. heavy cream, whipped
    1 angel food cake
    Coconut for garnish

Soften gelatin in cold water and set aside. Combine boiling water, juices, sugar and salt. Refrigerate until slightly thickened. Stir gelating mixture into whipped cream. Fold in orange juice mixture. Tear angel food cake in chunks. Layer cake and whipped cream mixture in a 9 x 13-inch pan. Garnish top with coconut. Refrigerate at least 6 hours or until ready to serve. Serves 12.

CARIOCA CUPS

    4 c. miniature marshmallows
    ½ t. salt
    ¼ c. milk
    1 6-oz. pkg. semisweet chocolate chips
    2 t. instant coffee
    ¼ t. cinnamon
    1 c. heavy cream, whipped
    8 sponge cake dessert shells
    1 c. finely chopped and whole pecans

Combine first three ingredients in the top of a double boiler. Cook and stir over boiling water until marshmallows are melted. Remove from heat and stir in chocolate chips, coffee, and cinnamon. Fold ½ cup of the chocolate mixture into the whipped cream. Cover and chill. Frost tops and sides of cakes with remaining chocolate mixture. Sprinkle nuts over. Spoon cooled filling in the center of the shells. Chill. Garnish with whole pecans. Serves 8.

VERY SPECIAL CARROT CAKE

    2 c. sugar
    1¼ c. vegetable oil
    4 eggs
    2 c. flour
    1 t. cinnamon
    ½ t. nutmeg
    1 t. salt
    2 t. baking soda
    3 c. grated carrot
    1 c. pecans
    ½ c. raisins
    1 c. crushed pineapple, drained

Cream sugar and oil. Add eggs, one at a time. Add flour, spices, salt and baking soda, mixing well. Add grated carrot, pecans, raisins and pineapple. Pour into a greased and floured 13 x 9-inch pan and bake in a 375° oven 50 to 60 minutes. Cool and frost with Cheese Icing. Serves 12.

CHEESE ICING

    1 8-oz. pkg. cream cheese
    ½ c. butter
    1 1-lb. box confectioners' sugar
    1 t. vanilla

Cream cheese and butter. Gradually add sugar, beating until fluffy and of spreading consistency. Stir in vanilla.

PINK DIVINE CAKE

1 pkg. white cake mix
3 T. flour
1 3-oz. pkg. raspberry gelatin
½ c. water
1 c. vegetable oil
½ 10-oz. pkg. frozen raspberries, thawed
4 eggs

Combine cake mix, flour and gelatin; mix well. Add water, oil, berries with juice and eggs. Beat well. Pour into 3 greased and floured 8-inch cake pans. Bake in a 350° oven 25 minutes. Cool 10 minutes. Remove from pans and ice. Serves 10.

Raspberry Icing

½ c. butter
1 1-lb. box confectioners' sugar
½ 10-oz. pkg. frozen red raspberries, thawed

Mix all ingredients together.

STRAWBERRY CAKE

1 pkg. yellow cake mix
2 c. fresh strawberries
1¼ c. macaroon crumbs
2 egg whites
Pinch cream of tartar
⅛ t. salt
1 c. strawberry jelly, slightly whipped

Mix cake according to package directions; bake in two 8-inch cake pans. Cool layers. Split cake layers horizontally to make 4 thin layers. Set aside a few berries for garnish. Mash remaining berries with a fork and let stand 10 minutes. Mix with cookie crumbs. Assemble layers, using strawberry filling between layers. Combine the egg whites, salt and cream of tartar. Beat until soft peaks form. Gradually beat jelly into the whites until stiff. Spread over tops and sides of cake and garnish with reserved berries. Serve immediately or refrigerate until serving time. Serves 10.

HOW TO SPLIT A CAKE FOR FILLING

Measure the cake with a ruler. Using toothpicks, mark into 3 equal depths. With picks as a guide and using a serrated knife, cut cake with a light sawing motion.

PEPPERMINT AND ICE CREAM CAKE

¾ c. round hard peppermint candies
¼ c. water
2 c. heavy cream, whipped
¼ c. confectioners' sugar
½ t. vanilla
1 angel food cake
1 pt. vanilla ice cream

In blender container, blend ½ cup candies on high speed until coarsely crushed. Remove to waxed paper. Blend remaining ¼ cup candies but leave in the blender. Add water; blend until syrupy. In small bowl with mixer at medium speed, beat cream, sugar and vanilla until stiff peaks form. Slice cake into 3 layers. Sprinkle bottom layer with 2 tablespoons peppermint syrup. Spread ½ cup whipped cream over the cake; sprinkle with 1 tablespoon crushed candies. Top with second cake layer. Sprinkle with syrup, spread with cream and sprinkle with candies as on the first layer. Invert top layer. Sprinkle cut side with remaining syrup. Place right side up on the cake. Spread remaining cream on top and sides of cake, dusting sides with crushed candies. With a small ice-cream scoop, scoop ice cream into balls. Place ice-cream balls on top of cake. Sprinkle with crushed candies. Freeze until served. Makes 10 servings.

CHERRY CHIFFON CAKE

1 lemon chiffon cake
1½ 8-oz. pkgs. cream cheese, softened
Grated rind of 1 lemon
¼ t. salt
1 t. vanilla
4 c. confectioners' sugar
½ c. chopped nuts
1 21-oz. can cherry pie filling

Cut cake into 4 layers. Combine cream cheese, salt, lemon rind and vanilla; beat until smooth. Add sugar, 1 cup at a time, beating well after each addition. Spread one-third of this frosting on the bottom layer of the cake and sprinkle with half the nuts. Top with second cake layer; spread with half the pie filling. Top with third cake layer and spread with one-third of the frosting; sprinkle with remainder of nuts. Add last cake layer, spreading top and sides with remaining icing. (Some of the icing can be set aside and used in a pastry bag to flute around the edge and center hole.) Spread remaining pie filling on top of the cake. Serves 16.

LEMON SPICE CAKE

1 pkg. yellow cake mix
1 3-oz. pkg. lemon instant pudding
1 t. cinnamon
½ t. ginger
¼ t. cloves
½ t. cardamom
¼ t. allspice
1 c. beer
4 eggs

Mix all ingredients together and beat until smooth. Bake in a 350° oven 45 minutes in a greased and floured tube pan. Remove from pan and pour glaze over cake. Serves 12.

GLAZE

1½ c. confectioners' sugar
2 T. butter
¼ t. lemon rind
1 t. lemon juice

Mix together all ingredients, stirring until smooth. If necessary, thin with a few drops water.

SWISS APPLE CAKE

1 pkg. German chocolate cake mix
1 21-oz. can apple pie filling
3 eggs
Whipped cream
Cinnamon

Blend cake mix with pie filling, and eggs. Beat 2 minutes at medium speed of electric mixer. Pour in a greased and floured 9 x 13-inch pan. Bake in a 350° oven 40 to 50 minutes. Serve with whipped cream and a sprinkle of cinnamon. Serves 16.

CITRUS CAKE

4 eggs
1 pkg. yellow cake mix
1 3-oz. pkg. lemon instant pudding mix
¾ c. water
½ c. buttery flavored oil
2 c. confectioners' sugar
⅓ c. orange juice
2 T. grated orange rind
Orange slices for garnish

Beat eggs. Add cake mix, pudding, water and oil. Beat 10 minutes. Pour into a greased and floured tube pan. Bake in a 350° oven 50 minutes. Cool. Combine sugar and orange juice; heat to boiling. Stir in orange rind and cool. Drizzle over cake. Garnish with orange slices.

PIÑA COLADA CAKE

1 pkg. white cake mix
1 3-oz. pkg. instant coconut cream pudding mix
4 eggs
½ c. water
⅓ c. dark rum
¼ c. vegetable oil

Blend all ingredients; beat 4 minutes at medium speed of electric mixer. Pour into 2 greased and floured 9-inch round pans. Bake in a 350° oven 25 to 30 minutes. Cool and frost with Pineapple-Rum Frosting. Serves 16.

PINEAPPLE-RUM FROSTING

1 8-oz. can crushed pineapple
1 3-oz. pkg. coconut cream instant pudding mix
⅓ c. rum
1 9-oz. container frozen whipped topping, thawed

Combine pineapple, pudding mix and rum. Beat until well blended. Fold in thawed whipped topping. Serves 16.

NUTTY ORANGE CAKE

1 pkg. orange cake mix
2 c. ricotta cheese
2 T. milk
1½ c. confectioners' sugar
¼ c. cut-up candied cherries
¼ c. candied lemon peel
¼ c. finely grated orange peel
¼ c. rum
1 envelope unflavored gelatin
¼ c. cold water
2 c. heavy cream
½ c. sugar
1 c. toasted and coarsely chopped pecans

Mix cake as directed on package and bake in two 8-inch layer cake pans. Cool, split each layer in half, making 4 thin layers. Beat cheese and milk until smooth. Gradually stir in confectioners' sugar. Fold in cherries, lemon and orange peel. Sprinkle each layer of cake with 1 tablespoon rum. Top 1 layer with one-third of the cheese mixture. Continue layering cake and cheese, ending with cake. Sprinkle gelatin over water. Set cup of gelatin in a pan of hot water and stir until dissolved. Cool slightly. Beat cream and sugar until fairly stiff. Slowly add cooled gelatin, beating to stiff peaks. Frost top and sides of cake; sprinkle with nuts. Serves 10.

EASY MANDARIN CAKE

1 box yellow cake mix
1 11-oz. can mandarin orange slices
4 eggs
½ c. vegetable oil

Combine all ingredients; mix for 2 minutes. Pour into 3 greased and floured 9-inch round layer pans. Bake in a preheated 350° oven 20 to 25 minutes. Remove from pans to wire racks. When cool, frost top and sides with Frosting. Serves 10.

FROSTING

1 9-oz. carton frozen whipped topping, thawed
1 20-oz. can crushed pineapple
1 3-oz. pkg. instant vanilla pudding

Combine all ingredients, mixing well.

POPPY SEED CAKE

1 pkg. white cake mix
¼ c. poppy seeds
1⅓ c. water
2 egg whites

Pour one-third cup water over poppy seeds. Let stand 30 minutes. Combine cake mix, egg whites, poppy seed mixture and remaining 1 cup water. Blend all and beat according to package directions. Bake in a greased and floured 9 x 13-inch pan in a 350° oven for about 30 to 35 minutes. Cool, fill and ice. Serves 12.

FILLING

½ c. sour cream
2 egg yolks
¼ c. milk
1 3-oz. pkg. vanilla instant pudding mix

Mix together the first 3 ingredients. Stir in pudding mix. Spread on cooled cake.

ICING

2 egg whites, room temperature
¼ t. cream of tartar
¼ t. salt
¼ c. sugar
¾ c. light corn syrup
1¼ t. vanilla

Add cream of tartar and salt to egg whites; beat at high speed of electric mixer until soft peaks form. Gradually beat in sugar until smooth and glossy. Gradually add corn syrup and vanilla, beating until stiff peaks form, about 7 minutes.

YELLOW MOON CAKE

1 pkg. yellow cake mix
1⅓ c. water
2 eggs
2 t. instant tea
Grated rind of 1 lemon
2 T. butter
½ t. cinnamon
2 T. brown sugar
1 3-oz. can chow mein noodles
⅓ c. apricot preserves

Combine cake mix, water, eggs, tea and grated lemon rind. Beat with electric mixer on high speed for 2 minutes. Pour into 2 greased and floured 9-inch cake pans. Bake according to package directions. Meanwhile, combine butter, cinnamon and brown sugar in a skillet. Heat until butter is melted. Add noodles and stir over low heat until syrup is absorbed. Cool. Coarsely crumble half of the noodle mixture; stir into apricot preserves. Use as a filling for the cake. Frost with a boiled icing. Garnish with remaining noodles. Serves 12.

> To produce a fancy marbled cake, remove half of the cake batter and set it aside. Add flavored gelatin powder to remaining batter and pour into the cake pan. Pour the reserved plain batter over flavored batter. Swirl by cutting through batter with a rubber spatula.

ALMOND CREAM MOCHA CAKE

1 pkg. chocolate cake mix
1⅓ c. water
2 eggs
3 T. instant espresso
1 3-oz. pkg. instant vanilla pudding
½ t. almond extract
1¼ c. milk
1 c. heavy cream, whipped
1 can cherry pie filling
Toasted almonds

Combine cake mix, water, eggs and espresso. Beat on high speed for 3 minutes. Pour batter into two 9-inch round pans and bake as directed on the package. Cool. Combine pudding mix, almond extract and milk. Beat until pudding thickens. Fold in whipped cream. Assemble cake, using pudding between layers and topping cake with cherry pie filling. Garnish with toasted almonds. Serves 16.

OLD-FASHIONED CHEESECAKE

1 pkg. active dry yeast
¼ c. warm water
1 T. sugar
½ c. butter, softened
2 c. flour
1 egg
½ t. vanilla

Soften yeast in warm water. In large mixer bowl, combine sugar, butter and flour. Mix until crumbly. Mix in softened yeast, egg and vanilla. Mix until a dough forms. Roll two-thirds of the dough to a 16 x 12-inch rectangle. Place dough in a greased 9 x 13-inch pan, pressing dough up the sides of the pan. Spread Pineapple Filling over, then carefully spread Cheese Filling on. Roll out remaining dough to a 9 x 13-inch rectangle, and place on top, sealing edges by pressing dough together. Cover and let rise in a warm place 60 minutes. Bake in a 375° oven 30 to 35 minutes. While warm, spread on Glaze. Cool. Refrigerate until served. Serves 14.

PINEAPPLE FILLING

3 T. sugar
2 T. flour
⅛ t. salt
1 13¼-oz. can crushed pineapple, undrained

Combine sugar, flour, salt and pineapple in a saucepan. Cook over medium heat, stirring constantly, until thick. Cool.

CHEESE FILLING

2 eggs
¾ c. sugar
2 T. flour
1 t. vanilla
2 c. creamed small-curd cottage cheese
1 8-oz. pkg. cream cheese, softened
½ c. flaked coconut

Combine eggs, sugar, flour and vanilla. Beat at medium speed until thick. Add cheeses and coconut, blending well.

GLAZE

1 c. confectioners' sugar
2 T. milk
½ t. white vanilla

Combine all ingredients and blend until smooth.

CHOCOLATE-FILLED ANGEL FOOD CAKE

1 1-oz. square unsweetened chocolate
1 king-size milk chocolate bar
1 c. butter
1 c. confectioners' sugar, sifted
4 eggs
1 T. creme de cacao
1 angel food cake
  Whipped cream

Melt chocolate in a double boiler; cool. Cream butter and confectioners' sugar. Add eggs, one at a time, beating after each addition. Add cooled chocolate and creme de cacao. Cut out inside of cake, leaving a ½-inch shell on sides and bottom. Lift inside out and set aside. Pour chocolate mixture into shell. Press cake which has been removed back into the chocolate center, allowing the chocolate to ooze over the sides. Refrigerate overnight or freeze. Serve with whipped cream. Serves 12 to 16.

FUDGY CHOCOLATE ICING

¼ c. instant hot cocoa mix
3 T. water
¼ t. salt
⅔ c. shortening
1 egg white
¼ c. cocoa
4 T. chocolate syrup
1 1-lb. box confectioners' sugar
1 t. white vanilla

Combine instant cocoa mix with water and salt. Beat until smooth. Add remaining ingredients, beating with an electric mixer 25 minutes. Add warm water, a teaspoon at a time, until of spreading consistency. Makes enough icing to fill and frost one 8-inch layer cake.

BOILED ICING

½ c. sugar
2 egg whites
2 T. water
1 7-oz. jar marshmallow creme
½ t. vanilla
  Food coloring (optional)

Combine sugar, egg whites and water in top of a double boiler. Beat with electric mixer over boiling water until soft peaks form. Add marshmallow creme and beat to stiff peaks. Remove from heat. Beat in vanilla and a few drops food coloring, if desired. Makes enough to frost a 10-inch cake.

Pictured opposite:
Cranberry Freezer Pie, p. 21

PIES

OIL PASTRY

2 c. flour
1 t. salt
½ c. vegetable oil
3 T. cold water

Toss flour and salt together. Add oil and mix with a fork until mixture looks like fine crumbs. Sprinkle with enough cold water to moisten. Gather into a ball with a fork. Roll out on floured board. Makes 2 single crusts or 1 double 9-inch crust.

PRETZEL CRUMB CRUST

1½ c. pretzel crumbs (use hard twisted pretzels)
½ c. sugar
¼ c. melted butter

Combine all ingredients, mixing well. Firmly press into the sides and bottom of a 9-inch pie pan. Bake in 400° oven 10 to 12 minutes. Makes one 9-inch pie shell.

PASTRY FOR ONE-CRUST PIE

1 c. flour
½ t. salt
1 T. sugar
⅓ c. shortening or lard
2 T. cold water

Toss flour, salt and sugar to mix. Cut in shortening with pastry blender or two knives until mixture looks like coarse meal. Sprinkle with water. Gather into a ball with a fork. Roll on a lightly floured board to a circle 1 inch larger than the inverted pie pan. Ease pastry into pie pan; fold edges under even with the pan rim. Flute edges. To bake before filling: prick pie shell with a fork. Bake in a 475° oven 8 to 10 minutes. Cool before filling. Makes one 9-inch pie shell.

COOKIE DOUGH PIE CRUST

1 c. flour
½ t. salt
2 T. sugar
½ c. butter

Toss flour, salt and sugar to mix. Add butter and work into a dough. Press into bottom and up sides of a 9-inch pie pan. Use for open-faced fruit pies. To use for chiffon and other cooked pudding pies: chill, prick and bake in a 400° oven 15 minutes or until golden brown.

FROZEN CRUST

1 c. creamed cottage cheese
⅓ c. sugar
1 t. vanilla
1 egg yolk
1½ pts. vanilla ice cream, softened

In blender, mix cheese, sugar, vanilla and egg yolk. Blend smooth. Stir into ice cream, mixing well. Place in freezer 45 minutes. Chill a 9-inch pie plate. Spoon mixture in and freeze 30 minutes. Using back of a spoon, spread evenly on sides and bottom of pan. Freeze solid. To serve, fill with sweetened fresh fruit. Makes one 9-inch pie shell.

GRAHAM CRACKER CRUST

1¼ c. graham cracker crumbs (19 crackers)
¼ c. sugar
6 T. melted butter

Combine all ingredients, mixing well. Press into a 9-inch pie pan. Chill 45 minutes for a chilled crust or bake in a 375° oven 7 minutes. Cool.

VARIATIONS

Peanut Butter Crust: Follow recipe for graham cracker crust, using only 4 tablespoons butter. Add ¼ cup creamy peanut butter. Mix well.

Spiced: To graham cracker crust; add 1 teaspoon cinnamon.

Orange: To graham cracker crust, add 1 tablespoon grated orange peel.

Nutty: To graham cracker crust, add ½ cup finely chopped nuts.

WALNUT CRUST

1¼ c. finely chopped walnuts
3 T. sugar
2 T. butter, softened
¼ c. unsifted flour

Combine all ingredients, mixing well. Press onto sides and bottom of a 9-inch pie pan. Bake in a 400° oven 8 to 10 minutes. Cool and fill. Makes one 9-inch pie shell.

HEALTH CRUST

¾ c. graham cracker crumbs
½ c. wheat germ
2 T. sugar
½ c. butter, softened

Combine all ingredients until well mixed. Press evenly into bottom and sides of a greased 9-inch pie pan. Refrigerate 15 minutes. Firmly press crust against pan. Bake in a 400° oven 8 to 10 minutes. Cool. Spoon in filling. Makes one 9-inch pie shell.

FESTIVE ICE CREAM PIE

1 c. M and M candies
2 T. butter
2 T. water
1 7-oz. can flaked coconut
1½ qts. peppermint ice cream

In a saucepan, combine M and M candies, water and butter. Cover and heat slowly 10 minutes, stirring smooth. Stir in coconut. Press against sides and bottom of a 9-inch pie pan. Chill. Scoop ice cream into the shell. Freeze. Serve with M and M Sauce. Serves 7.

M AND M SAUCE

1 c. M and M peanut candies
½ c. light cream
¼ c. light corn syrup
⅛ t. cream of tartar

Combine candies, cream, corn syrup and cream of tartar in a saucepan. Cover. Place over low heat 10 minutes. Uncover and stir until smooth. Chill. Thin with light cream if necessary. Serves 7.

NUT CRUST

3 oz. semisweet chocolate
2 T. butter
1¼ c. blanched almonds, toasted and finely chopped

Melt chocolate and butter over low heat. Stir in nuts, coating well. Refrigerate about 35 minutes. Spoon into a greased 9-inch pie pan. Press against bottom and sides. Refrigerate 2 hours before filling. Before serving, dip pan in hot water for 10 seconds, and serve at once. Makes one 9-inch pie shell.

CRANBERRY FREEZER PIE

1¼ c. cinnamon-graham cracker crumbs
6 T. melted butter
1 8-oz. pkg. cream cheese, softened
½ t. vanilla
1 c. heavy cream
¼ c. sugar
1 16-oz. can whole cranberry sauce

Combine crumbs and butter. Press into the bottom and up the sides of a 9-inch pie pan. Chill. Beat cheese and vanilla until fluffy. Whip cream, sugar, cheese, beating until smooth and creamy. Set aside a few whole cranberries for garnish. Fold remaining sauce into cream mixture. Pour into crust and freeze firm. Remove from freezer 10 minutes before serving. Garnish with reserved cranberries and additional whipped cream. Serves 10 to 12.

PUFFY PEANUT PIE

1 8-oz. pkg. cream cheese, softened
1 c. crunchy peanut butter
1 14-oz. can sweetened condensed milk
¼ c. lemon juice
1 t. vanilla
1 4½-oz. container whipped topping, thawed
1 graham cracker crust
Chopped peanuts for garnish

Cream cheese until fluffy. Beat in peanut butter and slowly add milk. Stir in lemon juice and vanilla. Fold in topping. Pour into the crust, garnish and chill 2 hours. Serves 7.

CHERRY PIE

1 9-inch graham cracker crumb crust
1 8-oz. pkg. cream cheese, softened
1 14-oz. can sweetened condensed milk
1/3 c. lemon juice
1 t. vanilla
1 21-oz. can cherry pie filling

Beat cheese until fluffy. Gradually add condensed milk, stirring well. Blend in lemon juice and vanilla. Pour into crust and refrigerate 3 hours. Top with pie filling. Serves 8.

STRAWBERRY CHEESE TARTS

24 ladyfingers
1 t. almond extract
1 t. vanilla
2 c. confectioners' sugar
2 8-oz. pkgs. cream cheese, room temperature
1 pt. heavy cream, whipped
1 3-oz. pkg. strawberry gelatin
1 c. boiling water
1 16-oz. pkg. frozen strawberries

Line a torte pan or a 9 x 13-inch glass pan with 24 ladyfingers. (Cut in half, lengthwise, to fit sides of pan.) Combine almond extract, vanilla, confectioners' sugar and cream cheese. Fold in whipped cream. Pour into crust. Dissolve gelatin in boiling water. Add strawberries, chill until slightly thickened. Pour over cheese mixture and refrigerate until ready to serve. Serves 12.

MAI-TAI PIE

2 c. flaked coconut
1/4 c. melted butter
1 8-oz. pkg. cream cheese
1 14-oz. can sweetened condensed milk
1 6-oz. can unsweetened orange juice concentrate, thawed
1/3 c. light rum
2 T. orange-flavored liqueur
1 4½-oz. container frozen whipped topping, thawed
Orange slices

Combine coconut and butter, mixing well. Press into the bottom and up the sides of a 9-inch pie pan. Bake in a 300° oven 25 minutes. Cool. Beat cheese until fluffy. Add milk and orange concentrate and beat until smooth. Add rum and liqueur. Fold in whipped topping. Pour into cooled crust and refrigerate 6 hours. Garnish with orange slices. Serves 7.

PUMPKIN CHEESE PIE

1¼ c. cinnamon-graham cracker crumbs
2 T. sugar
1 t. cinnamon
1/4 c. melted butter
1 8-oz. pkg. cream cheese
3/4 c. sugar
2 T. flour
1 t. cinnamon
1/4 t. nutmeg
1/4 t. ginger
1 t. grated lemon peel
1 t. grated orange peel
1/4 t. vanilla
1 16-oz. can pumpkin
3 eggs
Salted pecans

Combine graham crumbs, sugar, cinnamon and butter. Mix thoroughly. Press mixture firmly into bottom and up the sides of a 9-inch pie plate. Bake in a 350° oven 10 minutes. Cool. In a large mixing bowl, blend cream cheese, sugar and flour. Add remaining ingredients and beat until smooth. Pour into crust. Cover the edge with a strip of foil to prevent excessive browning. Bake in a 350° oven 50 to 55 minutes or until a knife inserted in the center comes out clean. Remove foil after 35 minutes of baking. Immediately spread on Topping. Refrigerate at least 4 hours. Garnish with salted pecans. Serves 8.

TOPPING

3/4 c. sour cream
1 T. sugar
1/4 t. vanilla

Combine all ingredients, mixing well.

DAIQUIRI PIE

1 9-inch graham cracker crust, baked and cooled
1 8-oz. pkg. cream cheese, softened
1 14-oz. can sweetened condensed milk
1 6-oz. can frozen limeade concentrate, thawed
1/3 c. light rum
Green food coloring
1 4½-oz. container frozen whipped topping, thawed
Lime slices

Beat cream cheese until light and fluffy. Add milk and limeade, beating smooth. Add rum and food coloring; fold in whipped cream. Pour into pie shell and refrigerate 6 to 8 hours. Garnish with slices of lime, if desired. Serves 7.

Pictured opposite:
Daiquiri Pie

CHOCOLATE BANANA PIE

1 c. vanilla wafer crumbs
½ c. chopped pecans
⅓ c. melted margarine
1 6-oz. pkg. semisweet chocolate chips
½ c. milk
3 c. miniature marshmallows
1 3-oz. pkg. vanilla pudding mix
1½ c. milk
½ c. heavy cream, whipped
2 bananas, thinly sliced

Combine crumbs, nuts and margarine; press into a 9-inch pie pan. Bake in a 375° oven 5 minutes. Combine chocolate chips, milk and 1 cup marshmallows. Stir over low heat until melted; pour into crust. Chill. Prepare pudding as directed on package, using 1½ cups milk. Cover with waxed paper and chill thoroughly. Fold whipped cream and remaining marshmallows into pudding. Arrange bananas over chocolate layer; pour pudding over bananas. Chill several hours. Garnish with additional bananas, whipped cream and chocolate pieces, if desired. Serves 6 to 8.

MILE-HIGH CHOCOLATE PIE

1 envelope unflavored gelatin
¼ c. cold water
3 1-oz. squares unsweetened chocolate
½ c. water
3 egg yolks
½ c. sugar
1 t. vanilla
¼ t. salt
½ c. sugar
3 egg whites, beaten stiff
1 9-inch baked pie shell
Whipped cream
Chocolate curls

Dissolve gelatin in ¼ cup cold water and set aside. In top of double boiler, combine chocolate and ½ cup water. Stir until blended. Remove from heat and add gelatin, stirring until dissolved. Beat egg yolks and gradually add ½ cup sugar, beating until light. Add chocolate mixture, vanilla and salt. Cool to room temperature. Gradually beat ½ cup sugar into beaten egg whites. Fold into chocolate mixture. Pour into pie shell. Chill until firm. Top with whipped cream and garnish with chocolate curls. Serves 7.

LEMONADE PIE

1 9-inch graham cracker crust
1 14-oz. can sweetened condensed milk
1 3-oz. can frozen lemonade concentrate
1 9-oz. container frozen whipped topping, thawed
Fresh slices of lemon

Chill milk; beat well. Add frozen lemonade concentrate; beat until thick. Fold in whipped topping and pour into the crust. Chill 1 hour. Will keep a week in the refrigerator. Before serving, top with lemon slices. Serves 7.

GRASSHOPPER CHEESE PIE

1 8-oz. pkg. cream cheese, softened
1 14-oz. can sweetened condensed milk
⅓ c. lemon juice
½ c. green creme de menthe
1 9-oz. container frozen whipped topping, thawed
1 9-inch graham cracker pie crust
Chocolate curls for garnish

Beat cheese until fluffy. Slowly add the milk, beating until smooth. Stir in lemon juice and creme de menthe. Fold in topping; pour into crust. Garnish with chocolate curls. Chill 2 hours. Serves 7.

POLKA DOT PIE

½ c. butter
¼ c. corn syrup
½ c. semisweet chocolate chips
2 c. cornflakes
1½ 8-oz. pkgs. cream cheese, softened
¾ c. sugar
2 T. brandy
½ c. maraschino cherries, drained and quartered
½ c. chopped pecans
2¼ c. whipped topping, thawed
Chocolate curls for garnish

In a saucepan, combine butter, corn syrup and chocolate chips. Melt over low heat, stirring constantly. Remove from heat and add cornflakes, stirring until well coated. Gently press into a well-buttered 9-inch pie pan. Chill. Beat cheese until smooth. Gradually beat in sugar and brandy. Fold in cherries, nuts and whipped topping. Spread onto crust. Garnish with chocolate curls. Freeze 4 hours. Let stand at room temperature 15 minutes before cutting. Serves 7.

TORTES

BUTTERSCOTCH TORTE

6 egg yolks
1½ c. sugar
1 T. baking powder
2 t. vanilla
1 t. almond flavoring
6 egg whites
2 c. graham cracker crumbs
½ pt. heavy cream, whipped
1 c. chopped walnuts

Beat egg yolks well. Combine sugar and baking powder; add to beaten egg yolks with flavorings. Beat egg whites stiff, but not dry. Fold into egg yolk mixture. Fold in cracker crumbs and nuts. Line two 9-inch pans with waxed paper and grease. Pour in mixture and bake in a 325° oven for 25 to 35 minutes. Cover with whipped cream and top with Butterscotch Sauce. Serves 8 to 10.

BUTTERSCOTCH SAUCE

1 c. brown sugar
1 T. flour
¼ c. butter
½ c. water
1 egg, beaten
½ t. vanilla
¼ c. chopped nuts

In a saucepan, combine first 4 ingredients. Cook over low heat or in top of double boiler until thick. Pour slowly over beaten egg, stirring constantly. Simmer another 2 to 3 minutes. Cool and add vanilla and nuts.

APPLE TORTE

1¼ c. flour
½ t. salt
1 t. sugar
1 t. baking powder
½ c. butter, softened
1 egg yolk
2 T. milk
3 to 4 apples, peeled and sliced

Sift together dry ingredients and combine with butter. Add egg yolk mixed with milk. Pat into the bottom of a lightly greased and floured 8-inch square pan. Arrange apples over crust. Top with Streusel. Bake in a 375° oven 45 minutes. Serves 6.

STREUSEL

¾ c. sugar
1½ T. flour
2 T. butter
¼ t. cinnamon

Combine ingredients, mixing thoroughly.

CHOCOLATE REFRIGERATOR TORTE

½ lb. box chocolate wafers, finely crushed
¼ c. melted butter
½ lb. marshmallows
⅓ c. milk
¼ c. maraschino cherry juice
¾ c. sliced maraschino cherries
½ c. chopped walnuts
½ c. heavy cream, whipped
Whipped cream

Pour melted butter over wafers; blend well. Press ¾ of the crumbs on the bottom of a greased 9 x 9-inch square pan. Melt marshmallows in milk and cherry juice in top of double boiler. Cool. Combine cooled marshmallow mixture, cherries, walnuts and whipped cream. Pour over crumbs. Refrigerate 3 to 4 hours. Cut in squares, top with whipped cream. Serves 8.

RED, WHITE AND BLUE DESSERT

1 can sweetened condensed milk
⅓ c. lemon juice
2 t. grated lemon peel
2 c. plain yogurt
2 c. miniature marshmallows
½ c. chopped pecans
1 pt. fresh strawberries, sliced
1 c. fresh blueberries

In a large bowl combine the condensed milk, lemon juice and lemon peel; mix well. Stir in yogurt, marshmallows and nuts. Spread half this mixture in a 9 x 13-inch dish. Place half the strawberries and half the blueberries on top. Repeat, using remaining fruit and yogurt mixture. Cover with foil and freeze. Remove from freezer 10 minutes before serving. Makes 15 servings.

STRAWBERRY TOPPED MERINGUE TORTE

6 egg whites
½ t. cream of tartar
¼ t. salt
1¾ c. sugar
½ t. almond flavoring or vanilla
2 3-oz. pkgs. cream cheese, softened
1 c. sugar
½ t. almond flavoring or 1 t. white vanilla
2 c. heavy cream, whipped
2 c. miniature multicolored marshmallows
2 to 3 pkgs. frozen strawberries, thawed

In a large bowl, beat egg whites, cream of tartar and salt until foamy. Gradually beat in 1¾ cup sugar (1 tablespoon at a time). Using high speed of mixer, beat until stiff and glossy. Add flavoring; mix well. Spread in a buttered 9 x 13-inch pan. Bake in a 275° oven for 60 minutes. Turn off oven and let cake set in oven at least 12 hours. *Do not open oven door.* Blend cream cheese, remaining sugar and flavoring until fluffy. Carefully fold in whipped cream and marshmallows. Spread over meringue. Chill 24 hours. Top with strawberries. Serves 12.

PRIZE-WINNING POTATO TORTE

1 c. butter
2 c. sugar
5 eggs
1 c. sour milk
1 t. baking soda
2 c. flour
1 t. cinnamon
½ t. cloves
¼ t. nutmeg
1 t. allspice
½ t. ginger
1 bar German sweet chocolate, melted
1 c. mashed potato (not instant)
½ c. chopped nuts
1 t. vanilla

Cream butter with sugar; stir in eggs. Combine sour milk and baking soda and add to butter mixture. Combine dry ingredients; beat in chocolate, potato, nuts and vanilla. Add to butter mixture. Pour into a greased and floured 10-inch tube pan. Bake in a 350° oven 60 minutes. Serves 16.

AUNT VIRGINIA'S RASPBERRY TORTE

1 c. flour
½ c. butter
¼ c. brown sugar
¾ c. chopped nuts
36 large marshmallows
1 c. milk
1 c. heavy cream, whipped
2 3-oz. pkgs. raspberry gelatin
2 c. boiling water
2 10-oz. pkgs. frozen raspberries

Combine flour, butter, brown sugar and nuts. Press into a 9 x 13-inch pan. Bake in a 350° oven 15 to 20 minutes. Melt marshmallows in milk; cool. Fold in whipped cream and spread on crumb crust. Combine boiling water and gelatin, stirring to dissolve completely. Chill until slightly thickened; add raspberries. Spread raspberry gelatin over top. Refrigerate overnight and cut in squares to serve. Serves 10 to 12.

COCONUT-STRAWBERRY TORTE

1 10-oz. pkg. frozen strawberries
2 envelopes unflavored gelatin
1 c. sugar
¼ t. salt
2 eggs, separated
3 8-oz. pkgs. cream cheese, room temperature
  Red food coloring
1 c. heavy cream, whipped
1 c. flaked coconut
  Fresh strawberries, sliced

Drain syrup from strawberries and set aside. In top of double boiler combine gelatin, ¾ cup sugar and salt. Beat together strawberry syrup and egg yolks and add to gelatin mixture. Heat over simmering water 10 minutes. Cool to room temperature and add thawed strawberries. Stir. Whip cheese until fluffy. Beat in strawberry mixture and food coloring. Chill. Stir occasionally until mixture mounds when dropped from a spoon. Beat egg whites until stiff but not dry. Fold into gelatin. Fold in whipped cream. Pour into a 9-inch round springform pan. Sprinkle with half the coconut. Chill several hours. When ready to serve, run knife dipped in hot water around the edge of pan. Press remaining coconut into sides and top of cake. Garnish with sliced strawberries. Serves 14.

Pictured opposite:
Coconut Strawberry Torte

CRANBERRY CREAM TORTE

1 c. graham cracker crumbs
¼ c. melted butter
2 c. cranberries
1 c. sugar
½ c. water
2 T. orange marmalade
¼ c. chopped nuts
1 8-oz. pkg. cream cheese
⅓ c. sifted confectioners' sugar
1 T. milk
1 t. vanilla
1 c. heavy cream, whipped

Combine crumbs and butter, mixing well. Press into the bottom of an 8-inch square pan. In a saucepan, combine cranberries, sugar and water. Bring to a boil. Simmer 20 minutes. Stir in nuts and marmalade, stirring to melt marmalade. Set aside and chill to be used as a topping. Combine cream cheese, sugar, milk and vanilla. Mix until well blended. Fold whipped cream into the cream cheese mixture. Spread on graham cracker crust and top with cranberry mixture. Chill until serving time. Serves 8.

BANANA SPLIT DESSERT

2 c. graham cracker crumbs
½ c. melted margarine
2 eggs
2 c. confectioners' sugar
½ c. margarine, softened
1 16-oz. can crushed pineapple
2 bananas
1 9-oz. container frozen whipped topping, thawed
Chopped pecans
Maraschino cherries

Mix graham crumbs and melted margarine. Pat into a 9 x 13-inch pan. Bake in a 350° oven 3 to 5 minutes. Beat 2 eggs, confectioners' sugar and margarine. Spread over crust. Drain pineapple, reserving juice. Cut bananas into ½-inch slices. Soak in reserved juice for 10 minutes; drain. Arrange drained pineapple and sliced bananas over second layer. Cover the banana layer with whipped topping. Garnish with nuts and cherries. Chill. Serves 12.

CHOCOLATE CHIP TORTE

10 eggs, separated
¼ t. salt
2 t. cream of tartar
1 c. sugar
1 c. sifted cake flour
1 t. vanilla
1 8-oz. bar German sweet chocolate, grated

Beat egg whites with salt and cream of tartar until foamy. Slowly add sugar and beat until stiff peaks form. Fold in flour, vanilla and grated chocolate. Beat egg yolks until lemon colored; fold into mixture. Pour into ungreased 10-inch tube pan. Bake in a 350° oven 60 minutes. Invert pan to cool. Split cake horizontally. Assemble cake, using Filling between layers and frost with Icing. Serves 12.

FILLING

½ c. butter, softened
1 6-oz. pkg. semisweet chocolate chips, melted and cooled
1 egg yolk
½ t. vanilla
2 t. cognac

Cream butter until fluffy. Beat in cooled, melted chocolate, egg yolk, vanilla and cognac. Refrigerate until of spreading consistency.

ICING

5 oz. milk chocolate
2¾ T. sugar
Pinch salt
3 T. water
3 egg yolks
½ pt. heavy cream, whipped

Cook chocolate, sugar, salt and water until smooth. Remove from heat and beat in egg yolks, one at a time. Cool completely. Fold in whipped cream.

To make chocolate curls or shavings, slightly soften chocolate candy bar with the heat of your hands. With a vegetable peeler, shave the narrow edge into curls.

MOCK CHEESE TORTE

2 c. graham cracker crumbs
2 T. melted butter
½ t. cinnamon
½ c. sugar
3 eggs, separated
1 can sweetened condensed milk
  Juice and rind of 1 lemon
2 c. applesauce
4 T. sugar
¼ t. salt

Combine cracker crumbs, butter, cinnamon and ½ cup sugar. Mix well. Set aside ¼ cup for garnish. Pat remaining mixture into a greased 10-inch springform. Beat egg yolks; add condensed milk, lemon juice and rind and applesauce. Beat egg whites until stiff; add remaining sugar and salt. Beat until soft peaks form. Fold into applesauce mixture. Pour into springform pan and sprinkle with crumbs. Bake in a 350° oven 50 minutes. Serves 10 to 12.

STRAWBERRY TORTE FLUFF

½ c. flour
¼ c. brown sugar
¼ c. margarine
⅓ c. chopped pecans
2 T. lemon juice
1 7-oz. jar marshmallow creme
1 16-oz. pkg. frozen strawberries, thawed
2 c. heavy cream, whipped

Combine flour and sugar; cut in margarine. Add nuts. Press into the bottom of a 9-inch springform. Bake in a 350° oven 20 minutes. Cool. Slowly add lemon juice to marshmallow creme. Mix until well blended. Stir in strawberries; fold in whipped cream. Pour over crumb crust. Freeze until serving time. Serves 8 to 10.

FREEZER MOCHA DESSERT

18 cream-filled chocolate cookies, crushed
⅓ c. melted butter
2 1-oz. squares unsweetened chocolate
½ c. sugar
⅔ c. evaporated milk
1 qt. coffee-flavored ice cream
1 c. heavy cream
¼ c. creme de cacao
  Shaved chocolate

Add melted butter to cookie crumbs and mix well. Press on bottom and up sides of an 8-inch springform pan. Bake in a 350° oven 8 to 10 minutes. Chill in freezer. Melt chocolate in top of double boiler; stir in sugar. Slowly add evaporated milk. Cook over low heat until thick, stirring occasionally. Chill. Let ice cream stand until soft. Spread ice cream over crust. Spread cooled chocolate mixture over the ice cream. Whip cream and add creme de cacao. Spread on top of torte and sprinkle with shaved chocolate. Freeze until served. Serves 10 to 12.

WAFER TORTE

1⅓ c. vanilla wafer crumbs
1 c. confectioners' sugar
½ c. butter
2 eggs
1 c. chopped pecans
1 15¼-oz. can crushed pineapple
½ pt. heavy cream, whipped

Grind wafers. Place half of crumbs into bottom of buttered 9 x 13-inch pan. Cream butter and sugar until fluffy. Stir in eggs, one at a time. Spread butter mixture on top of crust. Top with a layer of chopped nuts. Add a layer of drained crushed pineapple, and a layer of whipped cream. Cover with remaining crumbs. Chill 24 hours. Cut and serve topped with whipped cream. Serves 10.

LEMON BISQUE

1⅔ c. vanilla wafer crumbs
3 T. confectioners' sugar
1 t. cinnamon
1 T. melted butter
1 3-oz. pkg. lemon gelatin
1 c. boiling water
  Rind of 1 lemon
½ c. sugar
3 T. lemon juice
½ t. salt
1 13-oz. can evaporated milk, chilled
1 10-oz. bottle maraschino cherries, drained

Combine crumbs, confectioners' sugar, cinnamon and melted butter; mix well. Press into bottom of a 10-inch springform. Dissolve gelatin in boiling water. Add lemon rind, juice, sugar and salt. Chill until slightly thickened. Beat milk until stiff. Add gelatin mixture and beat an additional 10 minutes. Fold in cherries and spread on crust. Refrigerate 24 hours. Serves 10 to 12.

PINEAPPLE TORTE
CRUST

2½ c. flour
1 t. baking powder
Pinch salt
1 c. margarine
3 T. sugar

Combine all ingredients, mixing well. Press into the bottom of a 15½ x 10½-inch pan. Bake in a 350° oven 15 minutes, until light brown.

FILLING

1 20-oz. can crushed pineapple
½ c. sugar
2 T. cornstarch
1 6-oz. pkg. vanilla pudding
2 c. milk
2 c. heavy cream, whipped
2 t. vanilla

In a saucepan, combine pineapple, sugar and cornstarch; boil until thickened. Cool and pour over crust. Make vanilla pudding according to package directions, using the 2 cups milk. Pour over pineapple filling; chill. Fold vanilla into whipped cream and spread over top of torte. Makes 25 servings.

PRETZEL TORTE

2⅔ c. crushed pretzels (8-oz.)
¾ c. melted margarine
3 T. sugar
1 envelope whipped topping mix
½ c. milk for topping
1 8-oz. pkg. cream cheese, softened
1 c. sugar
1 6-oz. pkg. strawberry gelatin
3 c. boiling water
1 16-oz. pkg. frozen strawberries

Combine first 3 ingredients and pat in a 9 x 13-inch pan. Bake in a 350° oven 10 minutes. Cool. Prepare whipped topping according to package directions, using the ½ cup milk. Combine cheese, topping and remaining sugar and spread on top of cooled pretzel base. Dissolve gelatin in boiling water. Chill until slightly thickened; fold in frozen strawberries. Pour over cream cheese layer. Sprinkle additional crushed pretzels over the top. Serves 12.

SHERBET TORTE

1 pt. orange sherbet, softened
1 3-oz. pkg. ladyfingers
1 pt. raspberry sherbet, softened
2 c. frozen whipped topping, thawed
1 c. miniature multicolored marshmallows
Toasted pecan halves

Stir orange sherbet until smooth and pour into a 9 x 5-inch loaf pan. Cover with 12 double ladyfingers placed end to end. Stir raspberry sherbet until smooth and pour over ladyfingers. Freeze until almost solid. Stir marshmallows into the topping and spread over the top. Freeze firm. About 1 hour before serving fill a large bowl with hot water. Quickly lower pan in and out of the water. Loosen loaf with a spatula. Invert on platter. Place pecans on top. Return to freezer until serving time. Makes 10 to 12 servings.

LINZER TORTE

1 c. unsalted butter
1 c. sugar
2 eggs
2 c. sifted flour
1 t. cinnamon
¼ t. cloves
1 c. finely chopped blanched almonds
1 T. lemon juice
1 t. vanilla
1 10-oz. jar red raspberry jelly
Confectioners' sugar

Cream butter and sugar and beat until fluffy. Add eggs and blend well. Sift together flour, cinnamon and cloves. Add to batter and mix well. Add nuts, lemon juice and vanilla. Mix until smooth. Spread half of the batter in the bottom of a greased 10-inch springform. Spread jelly over the batter. Place remaining batter in a pastry bag that has a half-inch tube. Pipe batter around the sides forming a 1-inch ring. With the remaining batter, pipe a lattice over the top. Bake in a preheated 325° oven for 55 to 60 minutes until pastry is golden brown. Remove from oven. Cool 10 minutes. Remove sides of form and cool completely. Sprinkle torte with confectioners' sugar. Serves 10 to 12.

VALENTINE'S DAY TORTE

2 c. sifted flour
1 T. baking powder
½ t. salt
1½ t. cinnamon
¼ t. cloves
1½ c. graham cracker crumbs
¾ c. butter, softened
¾ c. sugar
4 eggs, separated
¾ c. milk
   Sliced almonds

Sift flour, baking powder, salt, cinnamon and cloves; stir in graham cracker crumbs and set aside. Cream butter with sugar until creamy. Add egg yolks, beating until light and fluffy. Stir in dry ingredients, alternating with milk, beginning and ending with dry ingredients. Beat egg whites until stiff, but not dry. Fold into graham mixture. Grease two 5½-cup heart-shaped pans; line with waxed paper and grease paper. Pour mixture into pans. Bake in a 350° oven 30 to 35 minutes. Cool in pans 10 minutes. Turn out on rack; peel off waxed paper. Cool completely. Split cake into 4 layers. Fill and frost with Chocolate Frosting. Garnish with sliced almonds. Serves 12.

CHOCOLATE FROSTING

½ c. butter, softened
2 eggs, separated
1½ c. confectioners' sugar
4 1-oz. squares unsweetened chocolate, melted

Cream butter until fluffy. Add egg yolks, beating until blended. Whip egg whites until foamy; gradually beat in sugar, beating until thick. Fold into butter mixture. Gradually stir in chocolate, blending well.

PUMPKIN CHEESE SPICE TORTE

CRUST

24 graham crackers, crushed
⅓ c. sugar
½ c. melted butter

Combine all ingredients, mixing well. Press into the bottom of a 9 x 13-inch pan.

FILLING

2 eggs, beaten
¾ c. sugar
1 8-oz. pkg. cream cheese
2 c. pumpkin
3 egg yolks
½ c. sugar
½ c. milk
½ t. salt
1 T. cinnamon
1 envelope unflavored gelatin
¼ c. cold water
3 egg whites
¼ c. sugar
½ pt. heavy cream, whipped

Combine eggs, ¾ cup sugar and cream cheese, mixing well. Pour over crust. Bake in a 350° oven 20 minutes. In a saucepan, combine pumpkin, egg yolks, ½ cup sugar, milk, salt and cinnamon; cook until mixture thickens. Remove from heat. Dissolve gelatin in cold water and add to pumpkin mixture; cool. Beat egg whites until foamy. Add remaining sugar and beat until soft peaks form. Fold into pumpkin mixture. Pour over cooled layer. Serve topped with whipped cream. Serves 8.

VIENNESE TORTE

½ c. butter
1 c. confectioners' sugar
1½ 1-oz. squares unsweetened chocolate, melted
3 eggs, separated
2 c. heavy cream, whipped
   Shaved chocolate
½ lb. vanilla wafers, crushed
1 c. chopped nuts

Combine butter, sugar, melted chocolate and egg yolks; mix until well blended. Beat egg whites until stiff; fold into chocolate mixture. In a 9-inch square pan, layer half the wafers then half the chocolate mixture. Repeat for two more layers and sprinkle with nuts. Top with whipped cream and garnish with shaved chocolate. Serves 8.

COOKIES

CHOCOLATE RAISIN COOKIES

½ c. shortening
½ c. brown sugar
¼ c. sugar
1 egg
½ t. vanilla
1 c. plus 2 T. flour
½ t. salt
½ t. baking soda
1 c. chocolate-covered raisins
½ c. coarsely chopped pecans

In a mixing bowl, with mixer at medium speed, cream shortening and sugars until fluffy. Mix in egg and vanilla. Sift together flour, salt and soda. With mixer at low speed, beat flour mixture into shortening mixture until smooth. Fold in raisins and nuts. Drop by spoonfuls onto greased cookie sheets. Bake in a 350° oven 10 to 12 minutes until lightly browned. Remove to wire rack to cool.

PEANUT DROPS

1 c. peanut butter
2¾ c. confectioners' sugar
½ c. butter, softened
¼ block paraffin
1 6-oz. pkg. chocolate chips

Cream peanut butter, sugar and butter. Roll into balls and stick with toothpicks. Refrigerate 2 hours. Melt paraffin and chocolate chips in a double boiler. Dip each ball into chocolate; chill. Makes 3 dozen drops.

GIANT CREAM-FILLED CHOCOLATE COOKIES

⅔ c. shortening
¾ c. sugar
1 egg
1 t. vanilla
2¼ c. sifted flour
1 c. instant chocolate-flavored mix
1 t. salt
½ t. baking soda
1 c. milk

Cream together shortening and sugar. Beat in egg and vanilla. Sift together flour, chocolate-flavored mix, salt and soda. Stir dry ingredients into creamed mixture alternately with milk. Drop by teaspoonfuls onto greased cookie sheets. Bake in a 400° oven 8 minutes. Cool on cookie sheet 2 to 3 minutes before removing. When cool, put 2 cookies together with Marshmallow Filling. Makes about 3 dozen cookies.

Marshmallow Filling

¾ c. butter, softened
2 c. sifted confectioners' sugar
2 c. marshmallow creme

Cream butter with sugar until light. Stir in marshmallow creme, blending well.

MOM'S CHOCOLATE CHIP COOKIES

½ c. butter
½ c. sugar
¼ c. brown sugar, firmly packed
1 egg, well beaten
1 c. sifted flour
½ t. salt
½ t. baking soda
1 6-oz. pkg. chocolate chips
1 c. coconut
1 t. vanilla

Cream butter and sugars until light and fluffy. Add beaten egg and mix thoroughly. Sift flour with salt and soda. Add flour in 2 parts to egg mixture and mix well. Stir in chocolate chips, coconut and vanilla. Mix well. Bake in a 350° oven 10 minutes. Makes 36 to 40 cookies.

CHERRY COBBLER BARS

1 pkg. yellow cake mix
¼ c. melted butter
2 eggs
1 21-oz. can cherry pie filling
1 pkg. coconut pecan frosting mix
2 T. melted butter

Combine cake mix, ¼ cup butter and eggs, mixing well. Pat into a 9 x 13-inch pan that is greased only on the bottom. Pour pie filling over, smoothing well. Combine frosting mix and remaining butter. Sprinkle over cherries. Bake in a 350° oven 30 minutes. Cool and cut into bars. Makes 24.

LEMON-CHEESE BARS

1 pkg. lemon cake mix
½ c. melted butter
1 egg, slightly beaten
1 pkg. lemon frosting mix
1 8-oz. pkg. cream cheese, softened
2 eggs

Combine cake mix, butter and 1 egg. Stir with fork until moist. Pat into a 13 x 9-inch pan, which has been greased on the bottom only. Mix cream cheese and frosting mix. Reserve ½ cup of the cream cheese mixture. Add remaining eggs to frosting mixture and beat 3 to 5 minutes. Spread over cake mixture. Bake in a 350° oven 30 to 40 minutes. Cool. Spread with reserved frosting. Makes 40 squares.

DAINTY COOKIES

2¾ c. sifted flour
1 t. baking soda
½ t. salt
1 c. butter
1 3-oz. pkg. gelatin, any flavor
½ c. sugar
2 eggs
1 t. vanilla
½ t. almond extract
½ c. milk

Sift flour, baking soda and salt. Set aside. Cream butter, sugar and gelatin until light and fluffy. Add eggs, one at a time, beating after each addition. Stir in flavorings. Add flour mixture, alternating with milk, and beating well after each addition. Drop by teaspoonfuls onto ungreased cookie sheets. Bake in a 375° oven 10 minutes, or until edges are lightly browned. Makes 5 dozen.

ORANGE BALLS

4 c. vanilla wafer crumbs
1 c. confectioners' sugar
1 c. finely chopped nuts
¼ c. melted margarine
1 6-oz. can frozen orange juice, thawed
Confectioners' sugar

Combine crumbs, sugar and nuts. Add margarine and mix well. Stir in orange juice. Mix well. Form 1-inch balls; roll in confectioners' sugar; refrigerate. Makes 4 dozen.

CLOUD PUFFS

5 egg whites
1 c. sugar
1 c. semisweet chocolate chips

Beat egg whites to soft peaks. Gradually add ¼ cup of the sugar; beat 3 minutes. Sprinkle remaining sugar over and fold in as gently as possible with a rubber spatula. Carefully fold in chocolate. Drop batter by spoonfuls onto a greased cookie sheet lined with waxed paper. Bake in a 275° oven 50 to 60 minutes. Puffs should be very dry and crisp. Makes 24 large puffs.

EGGNOG BARS

½ c. margarine, softened
1 c. sugar
1 t. rum flavoring
2¼ c. flour
1 t. baking soda
¼ t. nutmeg
¼ t. salt
1 c. eggnog
1 c. chopped maraschino cherries
½ c. chopped toasted almonds

Cream margarine and sugar until fluffy. Blend in rum flavoring. Combine flour, soda, nutmeg and salt. Add alternately with eggnog. Stir in cherries and nuts. Spread in a greased 15 x 10-inch jelly-roll pan. Bake in a 350° oven 18 to 20 minutes. Drizzle Icing over warm cake. Cool and cut into 48 bars.

ICING

¾ c. sifted confectioners' sugar
½ t. rum flavoring
3 to 4 t. milk
Green food coloring

Mix all ingredients until smooth.

Pictured opposite:
Cherry Cobbler Bars
Eggnog Bars

DREAMY CHOCOLATE BROWNIES

1¼ c. flour
½ t. salt
1 c. shortening
4 1-oz. squares unsweetened chocolate
2 c. sugar
4 eggs, well beaten
1 t. vanilla
1 c. chopped nuts

Sift together flour and salt. Set aside. In top of double boiler, melt shortening and chocolate. Add sugar, mixing well. Stir in eggs and vanilla. Gradually add flour and salt, stirring well. Remove from heat and add nuts. Spread batter in a well-greased 8 x 12-inch baking dish. Bake in a 400° oven for 18 minutes. Cool and frost with Chocolate Icing. Makes 32 servings.

CHOCOLATE ICING

2 1-oz. squares unsweetened chocolate
3 T. hot water
1 T. butter
2 c. sifted confectioners' sugar
½ t. vanilla
1 egg, beaten

Combine chocolate and hot water in top of double boiler. Heat, stirring, until chocolate is melted. Blend in butter; cool slightly and stir in confectioners' sugar and vanilla. Beat in egg. Spread on cooled cake.

PRETZELS A LA BROWNIE

⅔ c. shortening
4 1-oz. squares unsweetened chocolate
2 c. sugar
4 eggs
1 c. pretzel crumbs
1 c. sifted flour
1 t. baking powder
½ t. salt (use only with unsalted pretzels)
2 c. coarsely chopped pecans

In a large saucepan, melt shortening and chocolate. Add sugar and eggs; beat until smooth. Add pretzel crumbs, flour, baking powder and salt, if needed, and nuts. Pour into a greased and floured 9 x 13-inch pan. Bake in a 350° oven 30 to 35 minutes until center is firm to the touch. Cool in pan and cut into squares. Makes 30 squares.

LEMON BROWNIES

½ c. butter, softened
1⅓ c. flour
¼ c. sugar
2 eggs
¾ c. sugar
2 T. flour
¼ t. baking powder
3 T. lemon juice
Confectioners' sugar

Combine first 3 ingredients. Mix on low speed of mixer about 1 minute. Press into an ungreased 8-inch square pan. Bake in a 350° oven 15 to 20 minutes; edges will be slightly brown. Combine remaining ingredients except confectioners' sugar. Blend well. Pour over partially baked crust and return to oven for an additional 18 to 20 minutes or until filling is set. Sprinkle with confectioners' sugar. Cool and cut into squares. Makes 20 servings.

MALT COOKIE BARS

1 1-oz. square unsweetened chocolate
½ c. shortening
¾ c. sugar
½ t. vanilla
2 eggs
1 c. sifted flour
½ c. chocolate malted milk powder
½ t. baking powder
¼ t. salt
½ c. chopped walnuts

Melt chocolate; cool. Cream shortening, sugar and vanilla until fluffy. Beat in eggs. Blend in melted chocolate and set aside. Sift together flour, malt powder, baking powder and salt. Stir into creamed mixture; fold in nuts. Spread in greased and floured 8-inch square pan. Bake in a 350° oven 20 to 25 minutes. Frost with Malt Frosting. Makes 32 bars.

MALT FROSTING

2 T. butter, softened
¼ c. chocolate malted milk powder
Dash salt
1 c. sifted confectioners' sugar
Light cream

Cream butter, malt powder and salt. Slowly beat in sugar. Add cream until of spreading consistency.

FUDGE SCOTCH SQUARES

1 6-oz. pkg. semisweet chocolate chips
1 6-oz. pkg. butterscotch chips
½ c. peanut butter
1 box coconut pecan or coconut almond frosting mix
1 can sweetened condensed milk

In a large saucepan, combine chips and peanut butter. Melt over low heat, stirring constantly, until smooth. Remove from heat and add remaining ingredients, stirring well. Spread into an ungreased 9-inch square pan. Chill 2 hours. Cut into 1-inch pieces. Makes 6 dozen. Store in refrigerator.

CHOCOLATE NUT LOGS

1 1-lb. box confectioners' sugar
1 3½-oz. can flaked coconut
1 c. chopped peanuts
1 t. vanilla
1½ c. graham cracker crumbs
½ c. crunchy peanut butter
1 c. peanut oil
4 T. shortening
3 8-oz. pkgs. chocolate chips

Combine all ingredients except shortening and chocolate chips. Mix well, kneading until smooth. Pinch off 1½-inch pieces and roll into a log shape. Melt chips and shortening in the top of a double boiler. Place logs, one at a time, into the chocolate. Turn to cover completely with chocolate. Lift out with a fork. Place on waxed paper. Refrigerate to harden chocolate; store in a cool place. Makes 65 logs.

SWEDISH ROSETTES

1 large egg
1 c. milk
1 c. flour
1 t. vanilla
Melted shortening for deep frying

Mix egg, milk, flour and vanilla until smooth. Heat shortening to 350°. Dip rosette iron into hot shortening, then into batter and again in fat. Fry about 45 to 60 seconds on each side. Remove from oil and drain on paper towels. Cool and sprinkle with confectioners' sugar. Makes 4 to 5 dozen.

DATE MALT BARS

6 T. melted butter
¾ c. brown sugar
2 eggs, slightly beaten
½ t. vanilla
¾ c. sifted flour
½ c. chocolate malted milk powder
½ t. baking powder
1 c. snipped dates
½ c. chopped walnuts
½ c. flaked coconut

Blend brown sugar and butter. Beat in eggs, one at a time, and vanilla. Stir in flour, malt powder and baking powder. Mix well. Fold in dates, nuts and coconut. Pour into a greased and floured 9-inch square pan. Bake in a 350° oven 25 to 30 minutes. When cool, ice; cut into bars. Makes 16.

ICING

1 T. butter, softened
1 c. sifted confectioners' sugar
2 T. chocolate malted milk powder
¼ t. vanilla
1 t. milk

Combine all ingredients and beat until smooth.

CARROT SPICE NIBBLES

1 c. butter
1 c. firmly packed brown sugar
2 eggs
1 t. vanilla
1 c. flour
1 t. baking powder
1 t. cinnamon
½ t. salt
¼ t. nutmeg
¼ t. cloves
2½ c. quick oats, uncooked
2 c. shredded carrots
¾ c. raisins
¾ c. chopped nuts

Cream butter and sugar until light and fluffy. Add eggs and vanilla. Combine flour, baking powder, cinnamon, salt, nutmeg and cloves. Add to sugar mixture, mixing well. Stir in remaining ingredients. Drop by rounded teaspoonfuls onto ungreased cookie sheet. Bake in a 350° oven 12 to 15 minutes. Makes 5 dozen.

COCONUT COOKIES

⅓ c. shortening
1 c. sugar
1 egg
1 egg yolk
1½ c. flour
1 t. baking powder
½ t. salt
2 T. milk
½ t. vanilla
½ t. lemon juice

Blend shortening, sugar, egg and egg yolk. Sift together flour, baking powder and salt. Add alternately with milk, blending well. Add vanilla and lemon juice. Spread ¼ inch thick on a greased cookie sheet. Cover with Coconut Meringue. Bake in a 325° oven 30 minutes. Cut in squares. Makes 4 dozen cookies.

COCONUT MERINGUE

2 egg whites
1 c. light brown sugar
½ t. vanilla
⅔ c. shredded coconut

Beat egg whites stiff. Beat in sugar, ½ cup at a time. Add vanilla and fold in coconut.

MARSHMALLOW NUT GOODIES

1 12-oz. pkg. chocolate chips
1 12-oz. pkg. butterscotch chips
1 c. peanut butter
1 10½-oz. pkg. miniature marshmallows
3 c. Spanish peanuts

Melt chips and peanut butter over low heat, stirring to blend. Set aside to cool. Add marshmallows and peanuts, mixing well. Pour into a 12 x 9-inch pan or cookie sheet. Cool and cut into squares. Makes 24.

CHOCOLATE CREAM DROPS

½ c. heavy cream
2 c. confectioners' sugar
8 oz. sweet cooking chocolate, melted

Mix sugar with cream. Bring to a boil. Boil 5 minutes, stirring constantly. Set pan in a dish of ice water. Stir to a soft dough that can be handled. Roll into balls and place on waxed paper. When firm, dip balls, one at a time and quickly, into the chocolate. Return to waxed paper. Chill until served. Makes 3 dozen.

SOUR CREAM DROPS

3¼ c. sifted flour
1 t. salt
½ t. baking powder
½ t. baking soda
1 c. butter
1½ c. sugar
2 eggs
1 t. vanilla
½ t. almond extract
1 c. sour cream

Sift together flour, salt, baking powder and soda. Set aside. Cream butter with sugar until fluffy. Beat in eggs, vanilla and almond extract. Add dry ingredients alternately with sour cream, blending well. Chill about 2 hours. Drop by level tablespoonfuls onto greased cookie sheets. Bake in a 375° oven 10 to 12 minutes. Cool and frost. Makes 6 dozen.

ALMOND FROSTING

¼ c. butter
2½ c. sifted confectioners' sugar
1 t. vanilla
½ t. almond extract
2 T. light cream
Toasted almonds

Cream butter and sugar until light and fluffy. Add remaining ingredients except almonds. Cream until smooth. Spread on cookies, topping each with a nut.

CRISPY FLAKY COOKIES

1¼ c. flour
½ t. baking soda
¼ t. salt
½ c. butter, softened
1 c. sugar
1 egg
1 t. vanilla
2 c. crisp rice cereal
1 6-oz. pkg. semisweet chocolate chips

Sift together flour, salt and baking soda. Set aside. Cream butter with sugar until fluffy. Add egg and vanilla, beating well. Stir in dry ingredients, cereal and chocolate. Drop by spoonfuls onto greased cookie sheets. Bake in a 350° oven 12 minutes. Cool on wire racks. Makes 3½ dozen.

Pictured opposite:
Coconut Cookies

PINEAPPLE COOKIES

½ c. shortening
½ c. brown sugar
½ c. sugar
1 t. vanilla
½ c. crushed pineapple, drained
1¾ c. flour
1 t. baking powder
½ t. salt

Cream shortening, sugars and vanilla. Add pineapple. Sift dry ingredients and add. Form into small balls and press onto a greased baking sheet. Bake in a 350° oven 8 to 10 minutes.

Cookies can be decorated with a bit of flavored gelatin before baking.

GRAHAM COOKIES

1 1-lb. box graham crackers
1 c. margarine
1 c. sugar
1 egg
½ c. milk
1 c. graham crackers, crushed
1 c. chopped nuts
1 c. coconut

Cover a 10 x 15-inch cookie sheet with whole graham crackers. In a saucepan, combine margarine, sugar, egg and milk. Bring to a full boil, stirring occasionally. Remove from heat and add cracker crumbs, chopped nuts and coconut. Mix well and pour over graham crackers. Frost with Icing and cut in bars. Makes about 45 bars.

ICING

2 c. confectioners' sugar
½ c. margarine
1 t. vanilla

Cream sugar and margarine until light and fluffy. Add vanilla. If necessary, add milk, 1 teaspoon at a time, until of spreading consistency.

PUDDING DROPS

1 3-oz. pkg. chocolate pudding
1 c. sugar
½ c. evaporated milk
1 T. butter
1 c. unsalted peanuts

Combine all ingredients except peanuts in a saucepan. Bring to a rolling boil. Lower heat and boil for 3 minutes, stirring constantly. Remove from heat and add peanuts. Beat candy with a wooden spoon until it starts to thicken. Drop by tablespoons onto waxed paper. Makes 34.

DAD'S FAVORITE SUGAR COOKIES

¾ c. shortening
1 c. sugar
2 eggs
1 t. vanilla or lemon extract
2½ c. flour
1 t. baking powder
1 t. salt

Mix together shortening, sugar, eggs and flavoring. Stir in flour, baking powder and salt. Chill 1 hour. Roll dough ⅛ inch thick on a floured board. Cut out, using a 3-inch cookie cutter. Place on an ungreased cookie sheet and bake in a 400° oven 6 to 8 minutes. Makes about 3 dozen.

CHEESY EASY SQUARES

1 pkg. lemon cake mix
½ c. melted butter
1 egg, slightly beaten
1 pkg. lemon frosting mix
1 8-oz. pkg. cream cheese, softened
2 eggs

Combine cake mix, butter and 1 egg. Mix with a fork until moist. Pat into the bottom of a 9 x 13-inch pan, greased only on the bottom. Blend frosting mix into cream cheese. Set aside ½ cup of this mixture, and add 2 eggs to the remaining cheese batter. Beat 3 to 5 minutes. Spread over cake mixture in the pan. Bake in a 350° oven 30 to 40 minutes. When cool, spread with reserved frosting. Cut into squares. Serves 24.

CREPES

BASIC CREPES

1½ c. flour
1 T. sugar
½ t. baking powder
½ t. salt
2 c. milk
2 eggs
½ t. vanilla
2 T. melted butter

Measure flour, sugar, baking powder and salt into a bowl. Stir in remaining ingredients; beat until smooth. Lightly butter a 6-inch skillet. Heat until butter is bubbly. Pour a scant ¼ cup batter into the pan. Quickly rotate the pan until the batter is evenly distributed on the bottom of the pan. Cook over medium-high heat 30 seconds, until the underside is slightly browned. Turn over and brown the other side, about 15 seconds. While warm, spread with applesauce, jelly, jam or sweetened strawberries. Roll up and sprinkle with confectioners' sugar. Makes 16.

THREE-EGG CREPE

3 eggs, slightly beaten
6 T. flour
¼ t. salt
1 c. milk
  Butter

Beat eggs, flour, salt and milk until smooth. Cover and chill 1 hour. Stir well before using. For each crepe, heat about ½ teaspoon butter in a 7-inch crepe pan over medium-high heat. Pour in a scant ¼ cup batter. Quickly tilt pan to distribute batter evenly over bottom of pan. When light brown on the bottom, turn and lightly brown other side. Makes 12 crepes.

CHEESE CREPES

1 8-oz. pkg. cream cheese, softened
1 T. butter, softened
⅓ c. sugar
½ t. vanilla
⅛ t. salt
1 t. grated lemon peel
¼ c. plumped golden raisins
12 Three-Egg Crepes
¼ c. heavy cream
  Confectioners' sugar

Cream butter, cheese, sugar, vanilla and salt until fluffy. Fold in lemon peel and plumped raisins. Divide evenly among crepes; spread. Fold crepes on 2 sides and roll up. Place side by side in a greased 9 x 13-inch dish. Pour cream over. Bake in a 350° oven 10 to 15 minutes. Serve with warm cream and sprinkle with confectioners' sugar. Makes 12 crepes.

Note: To plump raisins, cover with hot water. Let stand 5 minutes and squeeze dry.

CREPES SUZETTE

⅔ c. butter
¾ t. grated orange rind
⅔ c. orange juice
¼ c. sugar
⅓ c. brandy
⅓ c. orange liqueur
12 Basic Crepes

In a 10-inch skillet, heat butter, orange rind, juice and sugar to boiling, stirring occasionally. Boil and stir 1 minute. Reduce heat and simmer. In a small saucepan, heat brandy and orange liqueur. Do not boil. Fold crepes into quarters. Place in hot orange sauce, turning once. Arrange crepes around edge of skillet. Pour warm brandy mixture in center of skillet. Ignite with match. Spoon flaming sauce over crepes. Place 2 crepes on each plate. Spoon sauce over crepes. Enough for 12 crepes.

SWEET CHERRY BLINTZES

2 17-oz. cans sweet cherries
2 T. flour
1 T. sugar
1 t. grated lemon peel
¼ t. cinnamon
18 Blintzes
4 T. butter
Sour cream
Cherry Sauce

Drain cherries, reserving 1 cup syrup for sauce. Carefully mix cherries with flour, sugar, lemon peel and cinnamon. Prepare blintzes. Place 1 heaping tablespoon cherry mixture on browned side of each blintze. Roll up, tucking in sides. Melt 2 tablespoons of the butter in a shallow 12 x 8-inch dish. Place blintzes side by side. Dot with the remaining 2 tablespoons butter. Bake in a 400° oven 10 minutes. Serve with sour cream and Cherry Sauce. Makes 18.

BLINTZES

2 eggs
1 c. milk
½ t. salt
¾ c. flour
2 T. vegetable oil
Butter

Beat eggs and milk. Add salt and flour; beat until smooth. Stir in oil. Chill 30 minutes. Lightly butter a 6-inch skillet. Pour in about 1 tablespoon batter, rotating skillet to coat bottom. Cook until pancake is lightly browned. Turn out, browned side up.

CHERRY SAUCE

1 T. lemon juice
1 c. reserved cherry syrup
1 T. cornstarch
1 t. water

Add lemon juice to cherry syrup. Dissolve cornstarch in small amount of water. Add to cherry syrup. Cook over medium heat until thick. Makes 1 cup sauce.

TROPICAL DELIGHT CREPES

3 eggs, beaten
⅔ c. flour
½ t. salt
1 c. milk

Combine all ingredients and beat until smooth. Let stand 30 minutes. For each crepe, pour ¼ cup batter into a lightly greased and hot 8-inch skillet. Rotate skillet to spread batter evenly. Cook until underside is lightly browned. Remove from skillet. Makes 8 crepes.

TROPICAL FILLING

1 7-oz. jar marshmallow creme
2 T. orange juice
¼ t. grated orange rind
1 c. heavy cream, whipped
2 bananas, sliced
2 8½-oz. cans crushed pineapple, drained
Toasted pecans

Combine marshmallow creme, orange juice and rind. Mix well. Fold in whipped cream. Spread ¼ cup of this on each crepe. Top with a few slices of bananas, and 2 tablespoons crushed pineapple. Roll up crepe. Serve with remaining marshmallow mixture. Top with pecans.

CHOCOLATE AND APRICOT CREPES

1 1-oz. square unsweetened chocolate
2 eggs
¼ c. sugar
1 t. salt
¼ t. cinnamon
1 c. water
½ c. light cream
¾ c. flour
Apricot jam
Confectioners' sugar
1 c. heavy cream, whipped

Melt chocolate. Beat eggs until thick and light. Gradually add sugar and salt, beating well. Blend in melted chocolate and cinnamon. Combine water with cream and alternately add to chocolate mixture with flour. Pour 2 tablespoons at a time into a hot, well-buttered 8-inch skillet; cook, turning once, until lightly browned. Set crepes aside. Repeat until batter is used up. Spread each warm crepe with 1 tablespoon apricot jam. Roll up and sprinkle with confectioners' sugar. Top with whipped cream. Makes 12 to 14 crepes.

HUNGARIAN CHOCOLATE CREAM CREPES

2 eggs
½ c. milk
½ t. vanilla
½ c. flour
1 T. sugar
⅛ t. salt
2 T. melted butter
Vegetable oil

In blender, blend eggs, milk and vanilla. Combine flour, sugar and salt; add to egg mixture. Beat until smooth. Blend in butter. Chill about 1 hour. Heat a 7 to 8-inch omelet or crepe pan over medium heat. Brush lightly with oil. Pour 2 tablespoons batter into pan, tilting pan to spread batter evenly. Cook until brown, about 1 minute. Loosen and turn; cook until lightly brown. Makes about 10 crepes. Place 3 tablespoons Cocoa Filling on each crepe and roll up as for a jelly roll. Top with Apricot Sauce. Refrigerate until served.

COCOA FILLING

⅓ c. cocoa
¼ t. salt
1 14-oz. can condensed milk
¼ c. hot water
2 T. butter
½ t. vanilla
1 c. heavy cream, whipped

Combine cocoa and salt in top of double boiler. Gradually stir in condensed milk. Place over boiling water. Stir constantly, until thick. Slowly stir in hot water. Cook 5 minutes, stirring frequently until thick. Remove from heat. Add butter and vanilla. Cool to room temperature. Fold whipped cream into chocolate mixture. Chill.

APRICOT SAUCE

1 17-oz. can apricot halves, drained (Reserve ½ cup syrup)
¼ c. sugar
4 t. cornstarch
¼ c. water
½ t. lemon juice
1 T. orange-flavored liqueur

Slice apricots and set aside. In a 2-quart saucepan, mix sugar and cornstarch. Gradually stir in reserved syrup and water. Cook, stirring constantly over low heat, until mixture thickens and boils. Add apricots and lemon juice. Heat until fruit is warmed through. Remove from heat and stir in orange liqueur. Serve warm. Makes 1½ cups.

HOT APPLE CREPE A LA MODE

8 crepes
1 20-oz. can apple pie filling with spice flavorings
¼ c. raisins
4 scoops ice cream
Chopped pecans

Combine pie filling and raisins. Mix well. Fill each crepe with 3 tablespoons of the mixture. Place in a 9 x 13-inch dish. Bake in a preheated 350° oven for 10 minutes. For each serving, top 2 crepes with a scoop of ice cream. Sprinkle with chopped nuts. Makes 4 servings.

CHOCO-CHERRY CREPES

8 crepes
1 4½-oz. pkg. chocolate instant pudding mix
1¾ c. milk
¼ c. cherry liqueur
⅓ c. chopped maraschino cherries
1 c. heavy cream, whipped
Whipped cream
Cherries

Combine pudding mix, milk and cherry liqueur. Whip until thickened. Stir in cherries; fold in whipped cream. Fill each crepe with about ½ cup of the mixture. Garnish with additional whipped cream and cherries, if desired. Serves 8.

ORANGE CREPES

⅔ c. flour
2 T. sugar
2 t. finely shredded orange peel
2 eggs
2 egg yolks
1½ c. milk
2 T. melted butter

Mix together flour, sugar and orange peel. Set aside. Combine eggs, egg yolks, milk and melted butter. Stir into dry ingredients, beating smooth. Lightly grease a 6-inch skillet. Heat skillet moderately hot. Remove from heat and spoon in 2 tablespoons batter. Rotate pan, spreading batter evenly over the bottom. Return to heat and brown one side only. Fill crepes with Orange Filling.

ORANGE FILLING

2 c. vanilla pudding
1 t. finely shredded orange peel
1 T. orange juice
2 egg whites
¼ c. sugar
2 T. orange juice
2 T. brandy

Combine orange peel and orange juice. Beat egg whites to soft peaks. Gradually add sugar, beating to form stiff peaks. Fold into 1 cup of the pudding. Spread 2 tablespoons Filling on each crepe and fold crepe in quarters. Place in ungreased 7 x 12-inch dish. Bake in a 400° oven 10 to 12 minutes. In a saucepan, stir remaining pudding, orange juice and brandy. Heat and pour over warm crepes. Serves 8 to 10.

AMBROSIA CREPES

4 crepes
1 16-oz. can fruit cocktail
1 c. frozen dessert topping, thawed
1 small ripe banana, sliced
½ c. miniature marshmallows
⅓ c. shredded coconut

Drain fruit, reserving 3 tablespoons of the juice. Reserve ½ cup fruit cocktail for garnish. Combine remaining fruit, dessert topping, banana, marshmallows, coconut and reserved juice. Mix lightly. Fill each crepe with ½ cup of the fruit mixture. Garnish with additional topping and reserved fruit. Sprinkle with additional coconut if desired. Makes 4 servings.

CHOCOLATE CREPES

3 eggs
1 c. flour
2 T. sugar
2 T. cocoa
1¼ c. buttermilk
2 T. melted butter

Beat eggs in a medium-size bowl. Combine flour, sugar and cocoa; add alternately with buttermilk. Beat until smooth. Beat in butter, refrigerate 1 hour. Drop 2 tablespoons batter on a lightly greased 6-inch skillet that is moderately hot. Rotate pan, spreading batter evenly over the bottom. Brown one side only. Fill with Almond Cream Filling. Makes 20.

ALMOND CREAM FILLING

1 c. sugar
¼ c. flour
1 c. milk
2 eggs
2 egg yolks
3 T. butter
2 t. vanilla
½ t. almond extract
½ c. ground, toasted blanched almonds
Melted butter
Grated unsweetened chocolate
Confectioners' sugar
Heavy cream, whipped

Mix sugar, flour and milk in saucepan. Cook and stir until thick, then cook and stir 1 to 2 minutes longer. Beat eggs and egg yolks slightly. Stir some of the hot mixture into the eggs, then return to hot mixture. Bring just to a boil, stirring constantly, and remove from heat. Stir in butter, vanilla, almond extract and almonds. Cool to room temperature or refrigerate if not using immediately. Fill crepes; roll up. Place, folded side down, in a buttered 9 x 12-inch dish. Brush crepes with melted butter. Heat in a 350° oven 20 to 25 minutes. Sprinkle with grated unsweetened chocolate. Sift confectioners' sugar over and top with whipped cream. Makes 20.

To freeze crepes, stack with waxed paper between. Wrap in heavy foil or freezer paper, sealing tightly. Will keep 3 months frozen. Thaw at room temperature. Heat in a 350° oven 10 to 15 minutes.

PASTRIES

COCOA CREAM PUFFS

1 T. cocoa
1 c. water
1 T. sugar
⅛ t. salt
7 T. butter
1 c. sifted flour
4 eggs
   Whipped cream
   Shaved chocolate

In a saucepan, combine cocoa, sugar, water, salt and butter. Bring to a gentle boil, melting butter. Add flour, all at once. Stir quickly with a wooden spoon until batter leaves the sides of the pan. Remove from heat and cool slightly. Add eggs, one at a time, beating after each addition. Dough will be smooth and glossy. If it is too soft, refrigerate 30 minutes. Butter cookie sheet and drop dough in 12 mounds. Bake in a 450° oven 10 minutes. Turn heat to 425° and bake 10 minutes, then turn heat to 400° for 10 minutes. Remove from oven and cool 5 minutes. Turn off oven. Cut tops of puffs with a serrated knife and remove them. Return to oven 15 minutes, leaving door ajar. Remove and cool thoroughly. Fill with Cocoa Cream Puff Filling. Garnish with whipped cream and shaved chocolate. Makes 12 puffs.

Cocoa Cream Puff Filling

1 c. semisweet chocolate chips
1 c. butterscotch chips
¼ c. milk
¼ c. sugar
⅛ t. salt
4 eggs, separated
1 t. vanilla

Combine chips, milk, sugar and salt in the top of a double boiler. Cook over hot water until mixture is smooth. Cool slightly. Add egg yolks, one at a time, beating well after each addition. Stir in vanilla. Beat egg whites stiff. Fold into chocolate mixture.

Pictured opposite:
Elephant Ears, p. 48

CANNOLI

3 c. sifted flour
¼ c. sugar
1 t. cinnamon
1 t. cocoa
¼ t. salt
3 T. shortening
2 eggs
4 T. red Italian wine
1 egg white, beaten
   Fat for deep frying
   Confectioners' sugar
   Pistachio nuts, finely chopped

Sift together dry ingredients. Cut in shortening, mixing well. Add eggs and wine. Knead by hand. Roll out to ⅛ inch thick. Cut in a circle. Wrap around metal cannoli forms; seal ends by brushing with beaten egg white. Heat fat to 350° and fry until slightly crisp (about 1 to 2 minutes). Cool on a paper towel. When cool, fill with Filling, sprinkle tops with confectioners' sugar and dip ends in finely chopped pistachio nuts. Makes about 3 dozen.

FILLING

3 lbs. ricotta
2¼ c. confectioners' sugar
1 t. vanilla

Beat ricotta smooth; add sugar and vanilla.

ALMOND KRANZ

2 T. sugar
3 c. flour
1 c. butter
1 t. salt
1 cake yeast
1¼ c. lukewarm milk
1 T. sugar
3 egg yolks
3 egg whites
1 c. sugar
1 c. chopped almonds
1 t. vanilla

Mix together 2 tablespoons sugar, flour, butter and salt. Set aside. Crumble yeast into a 1-cup measure; add ¼ cup lukewarm milk and 1 tablespoon sugar. Let rise to a cup. Beat egg yolks and remaining 1 cup milk. Add egg yolk mixture with yeast to flour mixture, beating well. Refrigerate overnight. Next day, on a floured board, roll dough out to about ¼ inch thick. Beat egg whites until stiff. Gradually add 1 cup sugar, beating to soft peaks. Fold in chopped nuts and vanilla. Spread egg white mixture over top. Roll up as for a jelly roll. Place in a greased 10-inch tube pan and pinch edges together. Let rise until doubled in bulk. Bake in a 350° oven 60 minutes. Makes 16 servings.

YULETIDE BUNS

1 pkg. hot roll mix
¾ c. warm water
1 egg
¼ c. sugar
½ c. brown sugar
3 T. melted butter
¾ c. chopped nuts
1 c. chocolate chips
½ c. confectioners' sugar
1 T. milk
Red diced cherries

In a large mixing bowl, soften yeast from the mix in warm water. Stir to dissolve. Blend in egg and sugar. Add dry hot roll mix, stirring until blended. Cover and let rise in a warm spot about 1 hour or until doubled in bulk. Combine brown sugar, butter and nuts in a small bowl; blend well. On a well-floured surface, knead dough lightly until no longer sticky. Divide dough in half. Roll each half into a 14 x 7-inch rectangle. Spread one-third of the filling on the dough. Sprinkle with half of the chocolate chips. Starting at longer side, roll up, pressing to seal edge. Cut roll into 1½-inch slices. Arrange rolls, cut side down, on a greased baking sheet. Cover and let rise in a warm spot 1 hour. Bake in a 350° oven 15 to 18 minutes. Combine confectioners' sugar and milk to make a thick glaze. Drizzle glaze over rolls. Garnish with cherries. Makes about 18 rolls.

TOFFEE SCHNECKEN

2 pkgs. active dry yeast
½ c. lukewarm water
1 c. lukewarm milk
½ c. butter, softened
⅓ c. sugar
2½ t. salt
1 egg, beaten
4¾ to 5¼ c. flour
½ c. butter, softened
⅓ c. sugar
1¼ c. chocolate-toffee candy chunks
½ c. chopped pecans
Corn syrup

Dissolve yeast in warm water. Add milk, butter, sugar, salt, egg and 2 cups of the flour. Beat until smooth. Stir in enough flour to make a stiff dough. Turn onto floured board and knead until smooth and elastic. Cover with plastic wrap and a towel. Let dough rest 20 minutes. Punch down dough. Cut into 2 equal parts. Roll each to a 12 x 9-inch rectangle. Cream butter and sugar. Stir in toffee and pecans. Spread half on each rectangle. Roll up tightly, beginning at wide side. Cut each roll into 12 even slices. Grease muffin tins and place 1 teaspoon corn syrup in each cup. Place slices in cups; cover with plastic wrap. Refrigerate 2 to 24 hours. Remove from refrigerator, uncover and let stand at room temperature while oven is preheating to 350°. Bake 20 to 25 minutes. Turn rolls out of pan to a rack to cool. Serves 24.

ELEPHANT EARS

1 pkg. dry yeast
¼ c. lukewarm water
2 c. sifted flour
1½ T. sugar
½ t. salt
½ c. butter, softened
1 egg yolk
½ c. milk, scalded and cooled
2 T. butter
1½ c. sugar
3½ t. cinnamon
1 c. chopped pecans
⅓ c. melted butter

Dissolve yeast in lukewarm water and set aside. Mix together flour, 1½ tablespoons sugar and salt. Cut in ½ cup butter. Combine egg yolk, milk and softened yeast. Add to dough, mixing well. Cover and chill at least 2 hours. Turn dough onto lightly floured board. Punch down. Cover with a towel and let rest 10 minutes. Roll to a 10 x 18-inch rectangle. Spread with 2 tablespoons butter. Combine cinnamon and sugar. Sprinkle ½ cup cinnamon-sugar mixture over dough. Roll up as for a jelly roll. Seal edges and cut into 1-inch slices. Dip slices, one at a time, in remaining cinnamon-sugar mixture. Roll out into 18 5-inch rounds. Sprinkle with a few nuts, pressing nuts in gently. Place on ungreased cookie sheets, brush with melted butter and sprinkle each with 1 teaspoon of the cinnamon-sugar mixture. Bake in a 400° oven 12 minutes. Cool on wire racks. Makes 18.

EVERYONE'S FAVORITE LONG JOHNS

1 c. milk
¼ c. butter
¼ c. sugar
1 t. salt
1 pkg. yeast
½ c. warm water
1 egg, beaten
3½ to 4 c. sifted flour
    Fat for deep frying

Scald milk; add butter and stir until melted. Add sugar and salt. Pour into a bowl and cool to lukewarm. Soften yeast in warm water and add to cooled milk mixture. Add egg and mix well. Gradually add flour, beating well after each addition, to form a dough. Knead on a floured surface until smooth and satiny—3 to 5 minutes. Place in a greased bowl and cover. Let rise in a warm place about an hour until doubled in bulk. Punch down dough. Cover and let rise again until light, about 30 to 60 minutes. Roll out dough on a floured board to a 12-inch square. Cut into 4-inch by 1½-inch rectangles. Place on a lightly floured surface and let rise, uncovered, 30 to 60 minutes until doubled in size. Heat fat to 375° and fry 1 to 2 minutes on each side. Dip tops in Maple Icing. Makes about 32.

MAPLE ICING

2 c. confectioners' sugar
2 T. butter
½ t. vanilla
¼ t. salt
¼ c. maple syrup

Combine all ingredients and mix until smooth. Add syrup until icing is of spreading consistency.

PUMP MUFFS

1 spice cake mix
1 c. pumpkin
⅔ c. water
2 eggs
1 6-oz. pkg. semisweet chocolate chips
    Whipped cream
    Pecan halves

Combine cake mix, pumpkin, water and eggs. Beat well. Stir in chocolate chips. Grease and flour 2½-inch muffin tins. Fill two-thirds full with batter. Bake in a 350° oven 15 to 20 minutes. Cool 5 minutes. Remove from pans. When ready to serve, top with whipped cream and a whole pecan half. Makes 24 to 30.

HOLIDAY PINEAPPLE CLUSTER BUNS

1 8½-oz. can crushed pineapple
1 pkg. active dry yeast
¼ c. warm water
2 large eggs
¼ c. syrup from pineapple
½ c. sugar
¼ c. melted butter
2¼ c. sifted flour
¾ t. salt
¼ t. nutmeg
¼ c. wheat germ

Drain pineapple, reserving syrup. Dissolve yeast in warm water; set aside. Beat eggs. Reserve 1 tablespoon beaten egg for glaze. Stir remaining eggs into the yeast mixture. Add ¼ cup syrup from the pineapple, ¼ cup sugar, melted butter and 1 cup flour. Mix well. Add salt, nutmeg and wheat germ. Gradually blend in remaining 1¼ cups flour, making a stiff dough. Cover bowl and set in a warm place for 1 hour. Place drained pineapple and any remaining syrup into a saucepan, add remaining ¼ cup sugar. Cook, stirring constantly, until thick. Cool. Punch down dough after 1 hour. Roll out on a floured board to a 9 x 12-inch shape. Cut into 3-inch squares. Set aside 1 tablespoon filling for the glaze. Divide remainder among the squares of dough. Fold the corners together to cover the filling. Pinch to seal and round up. Place seam side down in a well-greased 9-inch layer pan. Cover and let rise in a warm place about 45 minutes. Brush with reserved beaten egg. Bake in a 350° oven 30 to 35 minutes. Cool 15 minutes. Spoon Pineapple Glaze over. Serve warm. Makes 12 buns.

PINEAPPLE GLAZE

1 T. reserved pineapple filling
¾ c. confectioners' sugar
    Warm water

Combine filling, sugar and a few drops water. Stir until of spreading consistency. If necessary, add more warm water.

To keep muffins from burning around the edges, fill one of the muffin cups with water instead of batter. Bake as directed.

DIET DESSERTS

DIET CRANBERRY DELIGHT

1 envelope unflavored gelatin
¼ c. cold water
1 pt. cranberry juice cocktail
1 t. liquid sweetener

Soften gelatin in cold water for 5 minutes. Heat cranberry cocktail. Add gelatin and stir to dissolve. Add sweetener. Pour into 5 individual molds. Chill. Each serving contains 65 calories. Makes 6 servings.

PUMPKIN SPICE TORTE

2½ c. sifted cake flour
3 t. baking powder
2 t. pumpkin pie spice
½ t. cinnamon
½ t. butter-flavored salt
6 egg yolks
⅔ c. diet margarine
1 c. canned pumpkin
¾ c. brown sugar, firmly packed
　 Sugar substitute to equal 2/3 cup sugar
6 egg whites
½ t. cream of tartar

Sift together first 5 ingredients. Set aside. Combine yolks, diet margarine, pumpkin, brown sugar, and sugar substitute; beat smooth. Gradually add dry mixture to pumpkin mixture, mixing well. Beat egg whites and cream of tartar until stiff. Gently fold pumpkin mixture into egg whites. Pour into a greased 10-inch non-stick tube pan. Bake in a 325° oven 60 minutes. Invert pan on rack to cool. Serves 16. Each serving contains 160 calories.

DIET APPLESAUCE CAKE

2 c. raisins
2 c. water
1 c. unsweetened applesauce
2 eggs
¾ c. vegetable oil
2 T. liquid artificial sweetener
2 c. flour
1 t. baking soda
1¼ t. cinnamon
½ t. nutmeg

Cook raisins in water until soft; drain. Add applesauce, eggs, oil and sweetener to raisins. Mix well. Add remaining ingredients. Mix well. Pour into a glass 9 x 13-inch pan greased with diet margarine. Bake in a 325° oven 45 minutes. Serves 16.

DIET STRAWBERRY PIE

½ c. water
½ c. instant non-fat dry milk powder
4 eggs
¼ t. salt
½ c. sugar
¼ c. flour
1 T. lemon juice
1 t. vanilla
1 1-lb. container small curd cottage cheese
1 qt. whole strawberries
1 9-inch graham cracker crust

Combine first 9 ingredients; blend in blender until smooth. Pour into graham crust. Bake in a 250° oven 60 minutes. Turn off heat and leave pie in oven 60 minutes. Remove and cool. Arrange whole berries on top and brush warm Glaze over. Serves 10. Each serving contains 177 calories.

GLAZE

1 T. cornstarch
1 c. water
　 Liquid artificial sweetener
　 Red food coloring

In a saucepan, combine constarch and water. Cook over low heat, stirring constantly, until thickened and clear. Add liquid sweetener to taste. Stir in a few drops red food coloring. Cool slightly.

Pictured opposite:
Diet Strawberry Pie

DIETER'S DELIGHT

1 pt. dry-curd cottage cheese
1 3-oz. pkg. orange gelatin
1 11-oz. can mandarin oranges, drained
1 small can unsweetened crushed
   pineapple, drained
1 4-oz. container frozen whipped
   topping, thawed
   Cherries for garnish

Place cottage cheese in a large bowl. Pour gelatin over and mix gently. Add pineapple and oranges. Mix gently. Fold in whipped topping. For dessert, put a scoop in a dish and top with a cherry. Cover and store in refrigerator. Whip gently before serving. Serves 8 to 10.

DIET MOLASSES COOKIES

1 egg
½ c. molasses
¼ c. sugar
1 t. lemon extract
1 t. baking soda
½ t. cream of tartar
1 t. liquid artificial sweetener
1 t. ginger
1⅔ to 2 c. flour

Mix all ingredients together. Roll out ⅛ inch thick and cut with 2 or 3-inch cookie cutters. Bake in a 350° oven until lightly browned. Makes about 3 dozen cookies.

Note: One teaspoon orange rind can be substituted for ginger.

DIET SPICE COOKIES

1¼ c. water
⅓ c. shortening
½ t. salt
2½ t. artificial liquid sweetener
½ c. quick rolled oats
2 t. cinnamon
2 c. raisins
½ t. nutmeg
2 eggs
2 c. flour
1 t. baking powder

In a saucepan, combine first 8 ingredients. Boil for 3 minutes. Cool. Add remaining ingredients, mixing well. Drop by teaspoonfuls on a greased cookie sheet. Bake in a 350° oven 15 to 20 minutes. Makes 5 dozen.

PECAN SURPRISE DESSERT

3 egg whites
¼ c. nonfat dry milk
¼ c. ice water
¾ c. granulated sugar substitute
1 t. baking powder
½ t. baking soda
1 t. vanilla
¾ c. finely chopped pecans
20 snack crackers, crumbled

Whip egg whites, dry milk and ice water until stiff peaks form. Add sugar substitute, baking powder, soda and vanilla. Fold in pecans and cracker crumbs. Spread in a lightly buttered pie pan. Bake in a 350° oven 15 to 20 minutes. Serves 12 at 95 calories each serving.

DIET SHERBET

1 14-oz. can evaporated milk, well chilled
2 T. liquid artificial sweetener
1 6-oz. can unsweetened frozen orange
   juice concentrate, thawed

Beat evaporated milk, slightly. Gradually add sweetener and orange juice. Blend well. Pour into 3 pint containers. Freeze. One cup equals 140 calories. Yields 3 pints.

DIET DOTTED COOKIES

¾ c. sugar
½ c. margarine
1 t. coconut flavoring
3 T. skim milk
1½ c. sifted flour
½ t. baking powder
½ t. salt
¾ c. coarsely chopped cranberries, drained
½ c. shredded coconut

Cream sugar, margarine and coconut flavoring until fluffy. Add milk, mixing well. Sift together flour, baking powder and salt. Add to sugar mixture. Fold berries into batter. Divide dough in half. Roll each half into a roll about 1½ inches in diameter. Roll each roll in shredded coconut. Wrap each roll in waxed paper and chill 8 hours. Slice thin. Place on ungreased cookie sheet. Bake in a 375° oven 12 to 15 minutes. Makes 60 cookies. Each serving contains 39 calories.

CANDY

ALMOND BARK

2 lbs. chocolate
1 c. sliced almonds

Melt chocolate over boiling water. Line cookie sheet with aluminum foil. Sprinkle nuts in a single layer on foil. Slowly pour chocolate over, spreading gently. Chill. Break into pieces. Makes 2 pounds candy.

PEANUTTY FUDGE

¼ c. white corn syrup
¼ c. honey
¾ c. chunky peanut butter
½ c. butter, softened
½ t. salt
1 t. vanilla
4 c. sifted confectioners' sugar
¾ c. chopped peanuts

Beat first 6 ingredients together until blended. Add sugar to make a stiff dough. Knead with hands to blend well. Knead in nuts. Press into a well-buttered 8-inch square pan and cool. Cut into squares. Makes 2 pounds.

FRENCH MINTS

1 c. butter
2 c. confectioners' sugar
4 1-oz. squares unsweetened chocolate, melted
4 eggs
1½ c. crushed vanilla wafer crumbs

Cream butter and sugar, beating until fluffy. Add melted chocolate and beat well. Add eggs, one at a time, beating well after each addition. Put a teaspoon of crumbs into the bottom of paper 2½-inch muffin containers. Fill muffin paper to the top, using about 3 tablespoons of the chocolate mixture. Put remaining crumbs on top of the chocolate mixture. Freeze. Makes 22 to 24 mints.

PENUCHE

4 c. brown sugar
1 c. milk
2 T. butter
1 c. coarsely chopped pecans

Combine brown sugar, milk and butter. Heat, stirring constantly, until sugar is dissolved. Allow to boil until mixture forms a soft ball (232°) when dropped into cold water. Remove from heat and cool. Add nuts, stirring until mixture is creamy and begins to thicken. Spread into a buttered 12 x 8-inch glass dish. Chill until firm. Cut into squares. Makes 6 dozen.

MARSHMALLOW PENUCHE

1 c. brown sugar
1 c. sugar
⅔ c. evaporated milk
2 T. butter
1 t. vanilla
½ of a 1-lb. bag miniature marshmallows
1 c. chopped nuts

Butter sides of a 4-quart pot. Combine sugars, milk and butter. Cook, stirring frequently, until mixture comes to a boil. Cook to the soft-ball stage (238° on a candy thermometer). Remove from heat and add nuts, vanilla and marshmallows. Stir until marshmallows melt. Pour into a buttered 9-inch square pan. Cool and cut into 36 pieces.

SPECKLED CANDY ROLLS

1 8-oz. bar milk chocolate
1 12-oz. pkg. chocolate chips
½ c. butter
1 c. chopped nuts
1 pkg. multicolored miniature marshmallows
1 16-oz. pkg. flaked coconut

Combine chocolate, chocolate chips and butter in top of a double boiler. Stir until chocolate melts. Cool slightly. Stir in nuts and marshmallows. Using 2 pieces of aluminum foil, place half of candy mixture on each piece. Roll candy into 15-inch logs; roll each log in half the coconut. Seal and chill. Candy will keep in the refrigerator indefinitely. To serve, slice into ½-inch slices. Makes 2 rolls.

WHITE CHOCOLATE CREAM FUDGE

3 c. sugar
1 c. evaporated milk
¾ stick butter
1 pt. jar marshmallow creme
12 oz. white chocolate, cut in small pieces
1 c. chopped pecans
1 4-oz. jar candied cherries (optional)

Bring sugar, milk and butter to a boil over low heat, stirring constantly. Cook to 237°. Remove from heat, add marshmallow creme, white chocolate, nuts and cherries. Stir until marshmallow creme and chocolate are melted. Pour into a 13 x 9-inch buttered pan. Cool before cutting. Makes 6 dozen.

CRACKER CANDY

2 c. sugar
½ c. milk
¼ lb. soda crackers, finely crushed
1 T. peanut butter
1 t. vanilla

Combine sugar and milk and bring to a boil. Add remaining ingredients and let stand for 5 minutes. Beat and pour into a buttered 8-inch square dish. Cool in refrigerator. Makes 16 squares.

CARAMEL CORN

Popped corn
½ c. margarine
½ c. brown sugar
½ c. corn syrup
½ t. vanilla
½ t. salt
½ t. baking soda

Butter a 9 x 13-inch baking pan and fill with popped corn. In a saucepan, combine margarine, brown sugar and corn syrup. Bring to a boil and boil 5 minutes. Remove from heat; stir in vanilla, salt and soda. Pour over corn and mix from the bottom. Place in a 250° oven for 50 to 60 minutes. Stir every 15 minutes. Pour onto waxed paper; spread out to cool. Makes 4 quarts.

NUTTY FUDGE

2 c. chocolate chips
1 14-oz. can sweetened condensed milk
1½ c. chopped nuts
1 t. vanilla

Melt chocolate chips in a double boiler. Add milk. Remove from heat. Stir in nuts and vanilla. Mix well. Pour into a well-buttered 12 x 8-inch glass dish. Let set overnight or until it is dry on top. Cut into squares. Makes 72 pieces.

HEALTHY CANDY

1¼ c. wheat germ
½ c. creamy peanut butter
2 T. cocoa
2 T. honey
1 t. vanilla
⅛ t. salt

In a large bowl combine 1 cup wheat germ with remaining ingredients, mixing with back of spoon. Sprinkle remaining wheat germ onto waxed paper. Form into about 70 balls, using ½-teaspoonful mix for each ball. Roll balls in wheat germ. Cover and refrigerate. Makes 70.

SEAFOAM

3 c. sugar
½ c. light corn syrup
⅔ c. water
½ t. salt
2 egg whites
1 t. vanilla
1 c. chopped nuts

Combine sugar, corn syrup and water and boil until thermometer registers to 240° or until mixture spins a thread when dropped from a spoon. Add salt to egg whites and beat until stiff. Slowly pour syrup into beaten egg whites, beating constantly. When mixture thickens, add vanilla and nuts. Drop from a spoon onto waxed paper. Makes 4 dozen.

54

DESSERTS

PARTY ICE-CREAM DESSERT

1½ c. crushed cornflakes
1 c. light brown sugar
½ c. chopped nuts
½ c. flaked coconut
1 c. melted butter
½ gal. Neapolitan ice cream, softened

Mix together all ingredients except ice cream. Pat half of the crumb mixture into a 9-inch square pan. Press ice cream on crust and top with remainder of the crumb mixture. Freeze. Serves 10 to 12.

PINK CLOUD RICE PUDDING

2 egg yolks, beaten
3 c. milk
3 c. cooked rice
⅓ c. sugar
¼ t. salt
2 T. butter
1 t. vanilla
½ c. chopped maraschino cherries

Beat egg yolks with ½ cup of the milk; refrigerate until needed. Combine rice, remaining milk, sugar, salt and butter. Cook over medium heat until thick and creamy, about 15 minutes. Pour egg yolk mixture over. Cook 2 minutes longer, stirring constantly. Add vanilla. Spoon into serving dishes and chill. Top with Icing and garnish with cherries. Serves 6 to 8.

ICING

2 egg whites
¾ c. sugar
½ t. cream of tartar
Dash salt
¼ c. maraschino cherry juice
¼ t. almond extract

Beat egg whites until stiff but not dry. In a saucepan, combine sugar, cream of tartar, salt and cherry juice. Bring to a boil. Gradually pour hot syrup over egg whites, beating constantly. Stir in almond extract.

NUTTY GREEN SALAD DESSERT

1 16-oz. can crushed pineapple
1 3-oz. pkg. instant pistachio pudding
1 c. miniature marshmallows
1 4½ oz. container frozen whipped topping
½ c. chopped pecans
½ c. chopped maraschino cherries

Combine pineapple and pudding; mix until thickened. Add remaining ingredients and chill. Serves 8.

LEMON FRUIT FREEZE

⅔ c. butter
⅓ c. sugar
3 c. crushed Corn Chex cereal
1 can sweetened condensed milk
½ c. lemon juice
1 can lemon pie filling
1 20-oz. can fruit cocktail, drained
2 c. whipped topping

In a saucepan, melt butter; stir in sugar. Reserve one-third cup crumbs for garnish; stir remainder into butter and sugar. Pat firmly into the bottom of a 9 x 13-inch pan. Bake in a 300° oven 12 minutes; cool. Combine condensed milk and lemon juice. Stir in pie filling and fruit cocktail. Pour over crust. Top with whipped topping and reserved crumbs. Freeze 4 hours. Remove 20 minutes before cutting. Makes 16 servings.

CRANBERRY CREAM

4 c. fresh cranberries
1 c. cold water
¾ c. sugar
1 3-oz. pkg. pineapple gelatin
¾ c. boiling water
1 c. heavy cream
¼ t. salt
1 c. chopped walnuts

Reserve 12 cranberries; place remaining berries in a saucepan. Stir in sugar and cold water. Bring to a boil over medium heat and cook until berries pop. Force cooked berries through a strainer. Place gelatin in a bowl and add boiling water; stir well. Add cranberry puree and chill in refrigerator until thickened. Whip cream with salt until soft peaks form; fold in nuts. Swirl cream mixture into thickened cranberry mixture, creating a marbled effect. Pour into a 1½-quart mold. Chill. Unmold when firm. Garnish with reserved whole berries. Serves 8 to 10.

NOEL TORTONI

1 qt. vanilla ice cream
¼ c. chopped toasted pecans
2 T. chopped red maraschino cherries
2 T. chopped green maraschino cherries
1 t. rum extract
1 t. vanilla
½ c. M and M candies
Jimmies and whole cherries
Whipped cream

Scoop ice cream into a cold bowl. Stir until smooth but not melted. Stir in pecans, cherries and flavorings. Fold in candies. Spoon into 2½-inch foil baking cups. Freeze. Garnish each with whipped cream, jimmies and a whole cherry. Serves 8.

ICE CREAM-PUMPKIN SQUARES

2 c. canned pumpkin
1 c. sugar
1 t. salt
1 t. ginger
1 t. cinnamon
½ t. nutmeg
1 c. chopped pecans, toasted
½ gal. vanilla ice cream, softened
36 gingersnaps
Whipped cream
Pecan halves

Combine all ingredients except gingersnaps. Mix well. Line the bottom of a 13 x 9-inch pan with half the gingersnaps; top with half of the ice-cream mixture. Repeat for a second layer. Freeze 5 hours. Cut into squares and garnish with pecan halves. Serve with whipped cream. Serves 18.

CHOCOLATE ANGEL FREEZE

1 6 to 8-oz. angel food cake
1 12-oz. pkg. semisweet chocolate chips
4 eggs, separated
¼ c. sugar
2 T. heavy cream, whipped

Line an 8-inch square pan with waxed paper. Cut cake into 1-inch cubes. Melt chocolate chips in top of double boiler. Remove from heat and cool to lukewarm. Add beaten egg yolks to chocolate mixture. Mix well and cool. Beat egg whites until soft peaks form. Gradually add sugar and beat to stiff peaks. Fold into chocolate with whipped cream. Layer chocolate mixture and cake cubes, beginning and ending with chocolate mixture. Cover and freeze. To serve, garnish with pecans and cut into squares with a serrated knife. Serves 12.

CHOCO-FREEZE

1¼ c. vanilla wafer crumbs
4 T. melted butter
1 qt. peppermint ice cream, softened
2 1-oz. squares unsweetened chocolate
1 t. butter
3 egg yolks, beaten
1½ c. sifted confectioners' sugar
½ c. chopped pecans
1 t. vanilla
3 egg whites

Mix wafer crumbs with melted butter. Reserve ¼ cup crumb mixture. Press remaining mixture into a 9-inch square pan. Spread with ice cream and freeze. Combine butter and chocolate and cook over low heat until melted. Gradually stir in egg yolks, sugar, nuts and vanilla. Cool. Beat egg whites until stiff. Beat chocolate mixture until smooth; fold in egg whites. Spread over ice cream. Top with reserved crumbs. Freeze. Serves 8.

A LA FRUITCAKE PUDDING

1 3-oz. pkg. instant lemon pudding mix
2 c. milk
4 slices fruitcake
Whipped cream

Prepare pudding mix as directed on package, using 2 cups milk. Break fruitcake into small pieces; fold into pudding. Serve in sherbet dishes. Garnish each with dollop of whipped cream. Serves 6 to 8.

PEANUT BUTTER TORTONI

⅓ c. creamy peanut butter
¼ c. sugar
1 t. instant coffee
1 t. vanilla
1 egg white
1 T. sugar
½ c. macaroon crumbs
⅓ c. chopped peanuts
1 c. heavy cream, whipped

Blend together peanut butter, ¼ cup sugar, coffee and vanilla. Beat egg white to soft peaks. Gradually beat in 1 tablespoon sugar until stiff peaks form. Fold into peanut butter mixture. Combine cookie crumbs and peanuts. Fold half of the crumb mixture into peanut butter mixture, then fold in whipped cream. Spoon into 6 small serving dishes. Garnish with remaining peanut and crumb mixture. Makes 8 servings.

FRUITY SHERBET

5 ripe bananas
Grated peel of 2 oranges
1 c. orange juice
½ c. lemon juice
2 c. sugar
3 c. cranberry-apple juice
3 egg whites

Mash bananas. Stir in remaining ingredients except egg whites. Pour into a 15½ x 10½-inch pan and freeze until mushy. Mix fruit mixture in mixer at low speed. Beat egg whites stiff. Gently fold into fruit mixture. Return to pan and freeze until mushy. Pour into a bowl and beat; return to pan, cover with foil and freeze. Set out 15 minutes before serving. Spoon into sherbet dishes. Serves 14.

CHOCOLATE ALMOND VELVET

⅔ c. chocolate syrup
⅔ c. sweetened condensed milk
2 c. heavy cream
½ t. vanilla
⅓ c. chopped and toasted almonds
Almonds for garnish

Combine syrup, milk, cream and vanilla. Chill well. Whip to soft peaks. Fold in nuts. Pour into a freezer ice-cube tray and freeze. Spoon into sherbet dishes. Garnish with almonds. Serves 8 to 10.

CHERRY CHEESECAKE PARFAIT

1 3-oz. pkg. instant vanilla pudding
2 c. sour cream
1 8-oz. pkg. cream cheese, softened
¼ c. sugar
2 t. almond flavoring
1 t. vanilla
1 can cherry pie filling
1 3½-oz. can flaked coconut

Combine pudding mix, sour cream and cream cheese; whip until smooth. Slowly stir in sugar and flavorings. Spoon into 8 parfait glasses, filling each half full. Add 1 tablespoon pie filling to each glass. Spoon remaining pudding over and top with another spoonful of pie filling. Garnish with coconut. Serves 8.

TROPICAL SLUSH PARFAIT

Pour tropical-flavored fruit punch into freezer trays. Freeze until mushy, stirring once. Pile in parfait glasses. Serves 8 to 10.

Pictured opposite:
Cherry Cheesecake Parfait
Tropical Slush Parfait
Frozen Fruitcake Salad, p. 60

PEACHY CREAM PARFAIT

1 16-oz. can sliced peaches
1 3-oz. pkg. peach gelatin
2 c. vanilla ice cream

Drain peaches, reserving syrup. Add enough water to syrup to make 1 cup liquid and bring to a boil. Set aside 6 peach slices for garnish. Dice remaining peaches. Dissolve peach gelatin in liquid. Add vanilla ice cream; stir until melted. Add diced peaches and pour into 6 parfait glasses. Chill about 30 minutes. Garnish with reserved peaches. Makes about 3½ cups.

LAYERED PEPPERMINT CHILL

12 marshmallows
½ c. chopped nuts
½ c. crushed peppermint canes
2 c. heavy cream, whipped
1 c. graham cracker crumbs

Cut each marshmallow into 6 or 8 pieces. Fold nuts, crushed canes and marshmallows into the whipped cream. Butter an 8-inch square pan. Line bottom and sides with half of the graham cracker crumbs. Spoon cream mixture into pan; sprinkle remaining crumbs on top. Chill 24 hours. Serves 9.

RASPBERRY PARFAIT

2 pkgs. frozen raspberries
2 3-oz. pkgs. vanilla pudding
⅛ t. salt
2 c. water
2 T. butter
1 c. heavy cream, whipped

Force raspberries through sieve to remove seeds. Reserve juice. Combine pudding mix and salt in a large saucepan. Add water and raspberry juice; mix well. Cook and stir over medium heat until mixture comes to a full boil. Remove from heat and stir in butter. Chill. Serve in parfait glasses. Garnish with whipped cream. Serves 8.

PEACH MOUSSE

1 c. mashed peaches, drained
½ c. sugar
½ pt. heavy cream, whipped
2 egg whites, beaten stiff
¼ t. almond flavoring

Add peaches and sugar to whipped cream. Fold in egg whites and flavoring. Freeze. To serve, spoon into sherbet glasses. Serves 6 to 8.

PINEAPPLE FLUFF

1 8½-oz. can crushed pineapple, drained
1 10-oz. bag miniature marshmallows
1 T. confectioners' sugar
1 t. vanilla
½ pt. heavy cream, whipped
2 medium-size bananas

Pour pineapple over marshmallows. Place bowl in a larger bowl filled with ice. Set aside for 3 hours. Add sugar and vanilla to whipped cream. Before serving, slice bananas and fold into whipped cream. Serve in sherbet dishes. Serves 6 to 8.

FLUFFY MARSHMALLOW WHIP

1 3-oz. pkg. strawberry gelatin
1 c. boiling water
1 c. cold water
2 c. frozen whipped topping, thawed
1 c. miniature marshmallows
1 8-oz. can crushed pineapple, drained
Fresh strawberries for garnish

Dissolve gelatin in boiling water. Add cold water and chill until slightly thickened. Set bowl of gelatin in a larger bowl of crushed ice. Whip until light and fluffy on medium speed of mixer. Add 1½ cups whipped topping, beating well. Fold in marshmallows and pineapple. Chill until partially set. Mound in serving dish and garnish with the reserved whipped topping and fresh strawberries. Serves 6 to 8.

BLACK CHERRY WHIP

1 16-oz. can pitted dark sweet cherries
Cool water
1 3-oz. pkg. black cherry gelatin
1 c. boiling water
1 2-oz. pkg. whipped topping mix
Milk
¼ c. mayonnaise
2 medium bananas, peeled and diced
Whipped cream and toasted pecans for garnish

Drain syrup from cherries and reserve. Add enough cool water to make a cup. Dissolve gelatin in boiling water. Stir in cherry juice. Chill 20 minutes. Prepare topping with milk as directed on package; beat in mayonnaise. Add this to thickened gelatin, mixing well. Fold in cherries and bananas. Spoon into a 1½-quart mold. Chill overnight. Unmold and garnish with whipped cream and pecans. Serves 8.

FROZEN YULE LOG

1 20-oz. can sliced pineapple
1 c. quartered maraschino cherries
⅔ c. slivered almonds, toasted
¼ c. honey
1 c. mayonnaise
2 c. heavy cream, whipped
Almonds
Mint leaves

Drain pineapple, reserving ¼ cup syrup. Combine reserved syrup with cherries, almonds, honey and mayonnaise. Fold in whipped cream. In a 2-pound coffee can, layer pineapple and whipped cream mixture. Cover with plastic wrap and freeze. To unmold, run spatula around the inside of can, cut around bottom of can and push log out. Sprinkle with additional almonds and garnish with mint leaves. Makes 12 to 14 servings.

WALKING SALADS

¼ c. honey
1 8-oz. pkg. cream cheese
1 c. sliced banana
1 10-oz. pkg. frozen raspberries, partially thawed
2 c. heavy cream, whipped
2 c. miniature marshmallows

Blend honey and cream cheese. Stir in fruit. Fold in whipped cream and marshmallows. Pour into eight 6-ounce paper cups. Insert a wooden stick in the center of each cup. Freeze until firm. Tear away paper cups and eat. Serves 8.

FROZEN FRUITCAKE SALAD

1 c. sour cream
½ of a 4½-oz. container frozen whipped topping, thawed
½ c. sugar
2 T. lemon juice
1 t. vanilla
1 13-oz. can crushed pineapple, drained
2 bananas, sliced or diced
½ c. sliced red candied cherries
½ c. sliced green candied cherries
½ c. chopped walnuts
Lettuce
Candied cherries

Blend sour cream, whipped topping, sugar, lemon juice and vanilla. Fold in fruit and nuts. Turn into a 4½-cup ring mold. Freeze overnight. Unmold onto a lettuce-lined plate. Garnish with additional candied cherries. Let sit 10 minutes before serving. Makes 8 servings.

NAPOLEON CAKE SLICES

½ recipe puff pastry
1 recipe Creme Plombieres
  Confectioners' Sugar Icing
⅛ to ¼ c. chocolate syrup

Roll out puff pastry to a 16-inch square about ⅛ inch thick. Trim with a sharp knife and cut into three 5 x 15-inch strips. Place strips on a greased cookie sheet. Prick all over with a fork and freeze 60 minutes. Bake in a 350° oven 25 minutes until golden. Fill layers with Creme Plombieres, and ice top with Confectioners' Sugar Icing. Fill a pastry bag with chocolate syrup. With a #2 writing tube and working quickly, pipe lines, 1 inch apart, across the cake. Pass blade of knife the length of the cake through the chocolate lines, giving a marbled look. Serves 10.

CREME PLOMBIERES

3 T. flour
⅛ t. salt
⅜ c. sugar
1 c. light cream
4 egg yolks, slightly beaten
1 t. vanilla
1 envelope gelatin
¼ c. cold water
1 c. heavy cream, whipped
1 T. cognac
1 T. Kahlua
1 1-oz. square unsweetened chocolate, melted

Mix flour, salt and sugar in a heavy sauce-pan. Blend in a little of the light cream and place on medium heat, stirring constantly. Add remaining light cream and stir until thickened. Stir a little into the egg yolks, then pour yolks into flour mixture. Heat until thick, but do not boil. Remove from heat and stir in vanilla. Set aside. To prevent a skin from forming, brush top with melted butter. Stir before using.

Add gelatin to cold water. Heat in the top of a double boiler until clear. Stir into cream mixture. Fold whipped cream into the entire mixture. Divide mixture in half. Stir cognac into 1 half. Stir Kahlua and chocolate into the other half.

CONFECTIONERS' SUGAR ICING

1 c. confectioners' sugar
1 t. white vanilla
  Water

Mix vanilla and water into sugar, adding water by the teaspoonfuls until of spreading consistency. Beat until smooth.

APPLE STRUDEL

½ recipe Puff Pastry
1 c. fine dry bread crumbs
¾ c. melted butter
3 large McIntosh apples, peeled, cored and sliced ¼ inch thick
½ c. sugar mixed with 1 t. cinnamon
⅓ c. raisins
⅓ c. sliced, blanched toasted almonds
  Melted butter
  Confectioners' sugar

Roll dough out on a floured board to ⅛ inch thick. Sauté bread crumbs in ½ cup melted butter. Brush pastry with a thin layer of remaining butter. Spread bread crumbs on two-thirds of the dough nearest you. Spread apples over crumbs. Sprinkle apples with a mixture of cinnamon and sugar. Dot with raisins and nuts. Roll up strudel, beginning with edge nearest apples and pulling it up over apples. Continue to roll to the end. Seal ends. Place on a greased cookie sheet, open edge down, and form into a horseshoe shape. Brush top with melted butter. Bake in a 425° oven 45 minutes until golden brown. When cool, sprinkle with confectioners' sugar. To reheat, bake in a 425° oven 10 minutes. Serves 12.

QUICK AND EASY PUFF PASTRY

1½ c. unsifted flour
1 c. butter
½ c. sour cream

Cut butter into flour until it resembles crumbs. Stir in sour cream. Turn onto a floured board and knead only until it holds together. Form into a ball. Flatten slightly. Place on waxed paper. Wrap airtight. Refrigerate at least 2 hours or overnight. Work with half of the dough at a time and keep the other half in the refrigerator until ready to use. On a board, with a heavy rolling pin, pound the dough to make it pliable.

Note: Use for recipes calling for puff pastry, such as Strudel and Napoleons.

Pictured here clockwise from the top: Peppermint Ice Cream Cake, p. 15, Cherry Cobbler Bars, p. 34, Eggnog Bars, p. 34, Daiquiri Pie, p. 22, White Chocolate Cream Fudge, p. 54, Cherry Cheesecake Parfait, p. 59, Tropical Slush Parfait, p. 59.

APPLE CRISP

5 or 6 McIntosh apples, peeled and
   sliced
1 c. sifted flour
1 c. sugar
1 t. baking powder
¾ t. salt
1 egg
⅓ c. melted butter
   Cinnamon
   Ice cream

Butter a 10 x 6-inch baking dish. Fill ¾ full
with apple slices. Mix together flour, sugar,
baking powder, salt and egg. Spread over
apples. Pour melted butter over and sprinkle
cinnamon over top. Bake in a 350° oven 30
to 40 minutes. Serve warm with ice cream.
Serves 6 to 8.

APPLE BROWN BETTY

4 c. soft bread cubes
½ c. melted butter
¾ t. cinnamon
⅛ t. salt
¾ c. brown sugar
4 c. peeled and chopped tart apples
   Ice cream

Mix the first 5 ingredients together.
Arrange alternate layers of apples and bread
mixture in a greased shallow 1-quart cas-
serole. Cover with foil and bake in a 375°
oven 1 hour. Remove foil for last 15 minutes of baking time. Serve with ice cream.
Serves 4.

CHERRY COBBLER

2 T. shortening
1 c. sugar
1 c. milk
2 c. flour
2 T. baking powder
2 20-oz. cans sour red cherries
   Additional sweetening to taste
   Ice cream

Cream shortening with sugar. Add milk.
Stir in flour and baking powder. Pour into a
buttered 9 x 13-inch dish. Sweeten cherries
to taste and pour over batter. Bake in a 350°
oven 20 minutes. Serve with ice cream.
Serves 8.

FRUIT COCKTAIL COBBLER

½ c. butter
1 c. flour
1 c. sugar
2 t. baking powder
¾ c. milk
1 17-oz. can fruit cocktail, drained
   Ice Cream

Melt butter in a 9 x 13-inch pan. In a bowl
mix flour, sugar and baking powder. Stir in
milk until smooth. Stir into pan. Spoon fruit
evenly over the batter. Bake in a 350° oven
45 minutes. Serve topped with ice cream.
Serves 8.

MINCEMEAT SNACKIN' COBBLER

1 18-oz. jar mincemeat with rum and
   brandy
1 14½-oz. pkg. coconut-pecan snack cake
   mix
1 egg
2 T. butter, softened
   Whipped cream for topping

Heat oven to 325°. Spread mincemeat in an
8-inch square pan. Mix together dry cake
mix, egg and butter until crumbly. Sprinkle
over mincemeat. Bake 45 to 50 minutes or
until light brown. Serve warm. Garnish
with whipped cream. Serves 9.

PEACH COBBLER

1 c. buttermilk baking mix
4 T. brown sugar
⅓ c. milk
1 29-oz. can sliced peaches, undrained
3 T. cornstarch
2 T. butter
½ t. ginger
   Dash salt
   Whipped cream

Mix baking mix, 1 tablespoon brown sugar
and milk. Set aside. In a 10-inch skillet,
combine remaining brown sugar, peaches,
cornstarch, butter, ginger and salt. Cook
over low heat, stirring constantly, until
thick and bubbly. Drop batter mixture by
tablespoonfuls into hot peach mixture.
Cook, uncovered, over low heat 10 minutes.
Cover and cook an additional 10 to 15
minutes until dumplings are fluffy. To
serve, spoon syrup over dumplings and top
with whipped cream. Serves 6 to 8.

INDEX